I Appeal to Scripture!

The Life and Writings of
Michael Sattler

ISBN 978-1-68001-027-5
Library of Congress Control Number: 2018910806

For additional titles and other material by the same author, contact:

Sermon on the Mount Publishing
P.O. Box 246
Manchester, MI 48158
(734) 428-0488
the-witness@sbcglobal.net
www.kingdomreading.com

Our Mission
To obey the commands of Christ and to teach men to do so.

About the Cover
The cover is a representation of Michael Sattler's trial. On the front cover, Michael Sattler faces the angry Eberhard Hoffman, while Count Joachim of Zollern, the presiding judge, looks on. On the back cover are some of the other judges (seated) and Klaus von Graveneck (soldier), who wrote one of the accounts of Michael's martyrdom.
Cover art by Peter Balholm.

Dedication

This series is dedicated to the Lord Jesus Christ,
the King of Saints.

This volume is also dedicated to my parents, Vincent and
Barbara Ste. Marie, with gratitude for their countless
contributions to my life and work.

Acknowledgements

To all those whose assistance has made this book possible and improved it in numerous ways, I extend my heartfelt thanks. First, all glory, praise, and honor to the Lord Jesus Christ, our great king and example.

Mike Atnip helped with research assistance in the early stages of the writing of this book, reviewed it once written, and designed the cover. His close companionship in the field of Anabaptist studies is deeply appreciated. C. Arnold Snyder, Joe Springer, John D. Roth, and Stephen Buckwalter also assisted my research in various ways.

For their invaluable help in reviewing earlier versions of this book, I thank Vincent, Barbara, and Matthew Ste. Marie, Nate Wickey, Dale Burkholder, Chester Weaver, Leonard Gross, Jonathan Mast, Edsel Burdge Jr., and Shane D. Curran. Jennifer Burdge copyedited the manuscript.

Permission to use translations of primary sources is gratefully acknowledged from the Mennonite Historical Society, MennoMedia, and the Ohio Amish Library. The Basel University Library scanned the original of Sattler's letter to Bucer and Capito and granted permission to use it. Dean Taylor gave permission to use his photos of Anabaptist historical sites in Europe. Peter Balholm did an incredible piece of art for the cover. Llewellyn Martin gave valuable feedback on the cover design.

To these and any I have missed, I extend again my sincerest thanks and pray that the Lord will reward you for your work for Him.

Cross Bearers

Series

The **Cross Bearers Series** is presented to acquaint readers with men and women who followed in Jesus' steps. Today's reader is inundated with biographies of those who professed Christ, but who did not teach and practice what Jesus taught and practiced.

One of Jesus' plainest teachings is that "whosoever doth not bear his cross, and come after me, cannot be my disciple." (Luke 14:27) Yet how often we are told that Jesus died on the cross for us so that we do not need to die! Peter tells us in I Peter 2:21, "For even hereunto were ye called: because Christ also suffered for us, leaving us an example, that ye should follow his steps."

Our "heroes" help define who we are and who we intend to be. Today's youth are in desperate need of role models who go beyond saying, "Lord, Lord!" While Jesus is the Ultimate Example, we can also learn from those who strove to imitate Him. We can learn from their mistakes, as well as from their glorious victory over self, sin, Satan, and the world through the power of the Spirit that worked in them.

The stories presented in the *Cross Bearers Series* will be drawn from various ages and churches. While "historical fiction" may be easier to read, these biographies will present the stories using a minimum of author imagination. However, the stories will be salted and peppered with other content (artwork, photos, and text sidebars) to capture the context of the culture in which they walked.

The ultimate goal of the *Cross Bearers Series* is to provoke all of us to follow these men and women as they followed Christ.

Contents

Timeline

1490	Estimated birth year of Michael Sattler
1500	St. Peter's of the Black Forest dedicates new church building
1512	Jodocus Kaiser elected abbot of St. Peter's; Sattler probably entered monastery about this time
1517	Luther's 95 Theses challenge incorrect teachings on indulgences
1518	Approximate year of Michael Sattler's election as prior of St. Peter's monastery
1519	Margrave Ernst invades St. Peter's
1524	May: Peasants' War begins
1525	January 21: First Anabaptist baptisms
	Mid-April: Black Forest peasants revolt afresh
	May 12: St. Peter's invaded by rebelling peasants
	May 23: Freiburg surrenders to peasants
	May/June: ? Michael Sattler leaves monastery
	November 6-8: Second Zürich Disputation on baptism; Sattler may have attended
	November 18: Sattler swears obedience to Zürich, released from prison
1526	March 7: Grebel, Mantz, and Blaurock sentenced to life imprisonment
	March 21: Grebel, Mantz, and Blaurock escape from prison
	Spring/early summer: ?Sattler living with Hans Kuenzi, learning to weave
	May/June: Michael Sattler baptized
	June: Sattler evangelizing north of Zürich

	Late December/early January: Sattler travels to Strasbourg; discusses spiritual topics with reformers; departs
1527	January 5: Felix Mantz martyred; George Blaurock banished from Zürich
	January: Sattler evangelizes in Lahr
	February 24: Schleitheim Confession adopted
	February: Michael and Margaretha Sattler arrested
	Spring: Michael writes farewell letter to church in Horb
	April: Schleitheim Confession found in Bern
	May 17-18: Trial of Michael Sattler and several other Anabaptists
	May 20: Michael Sattler executed
	May?: Margaretha Sattler executed
	July: Ulrich Zwingli writes refutation of Schleitheim Confession
c. 1530	Schleitheim Confession printed in German
c. 1543	Schleitheim Confession printed in French
1544	John Calvin writes refutation of Schleitheim Confession
1560	Schleitheim Confession printed in Dutch

Others, indeed, who compose historical narratives, would record nothing but victories in battle, the trophies of enemies, the warlike achievements of generals, the bravery of soldiers, sullied with blood and innumerable murders, for the sake of children and country and property. But our narrative embraces that conversation and conduct which is acceptable to God, the wars and conflicts of a most pacific character, whose ultimate tendency is to establish the peace of the soul as well as those who have manfully contended for the truth rather than for their country and who have struggled for piety rather than their dearest friends. Such as these our narrative would engrave on imperishable monuments. The firmness of the champions for the true religion, their fortitude in the endurance of innumerable trials, their trophies erected over demoniac agency, their victories over their invisible antagonists, and the crowns that have been placed upon all these, it would proclaim and perpetuate by an everlasting remembrance.

—*Eusebius of Caesarea*
"The Father of Church History"

Part 1

The Life of Michael Sattler (c. 1490-1527)

1

The Anabaptist Mess

isintegration threatened the nearly two-year old Anabaptist movement in 1526 in Switzerland and southern Germany. Quarrelling individuals manifested bizarre behavior and theology. Catholic and Protestant authorities persecuted the movement ruthlessly. It must have seemed unlikely that Anabaptism could survive much longer. It was a moment of great crisis—and great opportunity.

Many months earlier, on January 21, 1525, the movement had begun at night, in a dimly-lit room in the home of Felix Mantz. There, a small group of about a dozen scholars and countryside pastors had met to pray and ask God for wisdom, direction, and strength to know and do His will, in spite of the opposition of foes. Those foes were not generic or abstract—they were Ulrich Zwingli, Leo Jud, and the Zürich City Council. That very day, the Council had published a decree forbidding this group to meet, forbidding them to continue discussing why infant baptism was unscriptural, and

1

ordering that all unbaptized infants be brought for baptism within eight days.

As the group prayed, George Blaurock—a radical ex-priest and a newcomer to the little band—rose and asked Conrad Grebel to baptize him on his faith and confession of the truth. With that, he fell on his knees before Conrad, and Conrad baptized him. The others then crowded around George, asking him for baptism and falling on their knees to receive the water. After baptizing each other, they appointed each other for the service of the gospel. The Anabaptist movement had been born.

Immediately following this nocturnal baptismal meeting, the dozen or so brothers became zealous missionaries, spreading the message of faith, salvation, and believer's baptism far and wide through Switzerland and even beyond the Swiss borders. In a short time, multiple Anabaptist congregations had arisen, both in areas which were officially Protestant and even in places still ruled by Catholic authorities. Beginning at Zollikon, a small village near Zürich, churches were established in St. Gall, Bern, Appenzell, Schaffhausen, Grüningen, Waldshut, Nikolsburg, and in the Tyrol.

Fierce repression followed and accompanied the vigorous growth. The three most prominent leaders—Conrad Grebel, George Blaurock, and Felix Mantz—spent their share of time sitting in Zürich prison cells. Ulrich Zwingli and the Zürich Council did everything they could to stop the movement, and on March 7, 1526, finally sentenced the three leaders and several other Anabaptists to life imprisonment on a diet of bread and water.

Theirs was a short life imprisonment. Only two weeks after their sentencing, they escaped from prison, and rather than settling down into comfortable, quiet lives, they immediately went back to the mission field to continue the labors interrupted by suffering.

The Anabaptist movement began on January 21, 1525, when Conrad Grebel baptized George Blaurock in Felix Mantz's mother's house.

They were to find that the fruit of their labors was not as they had left it. The movement in Grüningen collapsed. In St. Gall and Appenzell, the Anabaptists were persecuted viciously, most recanted, and the remnants descended into bizarre forms of behavior. With growth came a divergence of multiple visions for the church. Balthasar Hubmaier and his followers supported the use of the sword for Christians. Some denied the validity of "outward signs" such as baptism and the Lord's Supper, and some even claimed that since the Spirit set them free from the "letter," the Bible itself was now superfluous—and they threw their New Testaments into the stove.[1] Some—perhaps influenced by Protestant theologians such as Martin Bucer and Wolfgang Capito—claimed that since they were "believers" and had "faith and love," they could do whatever they pleased, without harm to their salvation.

---

1   Literally, according to Johannes Kessler's *Sabbata*. Leland Harder, editor, *The Sources of Swiss Anabaptism*, 1985, Herald Press, pp. 455-456.

Veterans from the lost cause of the Peasants' War were joining the Anabaptist movement, with varying degrees of conviction (or lack thereof) for nonresistance. Some, such as Hans Hut, taught secret doctrines to special "mature" converts—doctrines about the end times, when the Anabaptists would supposedly take bloody vengeance on the authorities. Anabaptism was a mess. Without the unifying force of a compelling and Scriptural vision, the movement threatened to degenerate and collapse.

Fleeing from their imprisonment in Zürich, Conrad Grebel and Felix Mantz together went to Appenzell and attempted to set the record straight with some Anabaptists who considered themselves too spiritual to keep reading the New Testament. Instead of meeting receptive hearts, however, they met with a group which lashed out at them, calling them "scribes" and "false prophets." Conrad Grebel traveled to Maienfeld, where his sister lived, and—weak from his prison experiences—died of the plague.

A few months later, Felix Mantz was again imprisoned, and was given a "third baptism"—drowning—in the Limmat River which flows through Zürich. George Blaurock was banished from Zürich.

Engulfed in persecution, embroiled in doctrinal disputes, and lacking adequate leadership, the Anabaptist movement needed a compelling vision and a man to personify that vision. Thankfully, God sent a man who stepped into the gap and filled that role. His name was Michael Sattler.

Benedict of Nursia wrote the
Rule of St. Benedict, *a guide for*
monastic life.

2
Cloister Lord

𝓘magine that you are living in the 400's, and you desire to live a serious and committed Christian life. Yet the post-Constantinian church is filled with carnal, worldly people—people who have no interest in following the teachings of Jesus, but are all considered good Christians nevertheless. What would you do to show your commitment to radical Christianity?

You could stay within the mainstream church and try to live a godly life within it, setting a good example and hoping to make a positive impact. While it was surely a lonely path, some did try to do this.

More likely, if you were really committed and wanted fellowship, you would become a monk or nun, living a life of prayer and service without marrying.

Monasticism (being a monk or nun) was a way to live out serious, committed Christianity, usually in a communal context. In this way, monastic movements were examples of a mindset of *ecclesiola in ecclesia*—a Latin phrase meaning "a little church within the church." Without officially breaking ties with the institutional church, the monks hoped to be a smaller, purer communion, showing to all an example of what Christianity was meant to be.

Throughout the Middle Ages, the character of monasticism as a haven for the spiritually serious continued—interrupted, sadly, by the apostasy of various specific monastic orders into spiritual and even moral laxity. Nevertheless, those who wished to live serious Christian lives in the Middle Ages often joined a monastery. Michael Sattler seems to have been one of these. When such earnest young people found the corruption existing within the monastery walls, they were often disappointed, and many Protestant and Anabaptist leaders were ex-monastics—including Martin Luther, Michael Sattler, and many others.

Because the monks and nuns were still in fellowship with the *ecclesia*, the "big church," and recognized its validity, a theology developed about the teachings of Jesus which said that they were "councils of perfection." Jesus had told the rich young ruler, "If thou wilt be perfect, go and sell that thou hast, and give to the poor, and thou shalt have treasure in heaven: and come and follow me" (Matthew 19:21). Thus, many medieval minds concluded, Jesus meant His most challenging teachings (such as those on wealth and nonresistance) to be for "the perfect," such as monks, nuns, and priests. These "spiritual" people needed to live by Jesus' higher ethical teachings, while there was a lower standard (the Ten Commandments) for the average Christian to live by.

With this theology, full obedience to the teachings of Jesus was effectively made optional. If one wanted to be one of "the perfect," he needed to obey them; if he only wanted to be an "average" Christian, he did not need to. Thus, there were two levels of people, two levels of commitment, two levels of righteousness, and two ethical standards permitted by the medieval church.[1]

Should the earnest, committed, spiritual people simply have left the institutional church and set up separate churches? From our perspective centuries later, we often think that would have been a better option. But from their perspective, dividing the church of Christ was unthinkable; only heretics—like the Gnostics, Ebionites, or Montanists—did things like that. It was better to try to form an *ecclesiola in ecclesia*—a little church still in fellowship (at least in theory) with the big one, serving as a good example of what Christianity is really supposed to be like.

Benedict of Nursia

One early Western leader of this movement toward a serious, monastic Christianity was Benedict of Nursia (c. 480-543 or 547 A.D.). Benedict was the son of well-to-do parents and was born in Nursia, northeast of Rome. His parents sent him to Rome to study, but while there, he was repulsed by the sinful lives of the "Christians" living there. He feared for his own soul, lest he should be drawn into the sinfulness of those around him. He therefore forsook his wealth

Benedict—a Western Leader?

Monasticism began in Egypt and Palestine. Benedict lived in Italy. He was not the founder of Western monasticism, but was very influential upon it.

---

1   For example, although the *Rule of St. Benedict* forbids oaths for monks (4:27-28), it requires an oath from some parents of minors being admitted to the monastery (59:3). Timothy Fry, editor, *RB 1980: The Rule of St. Benedict in English*, 1982, The Liturgical Press, pp. 27, 81.

and his family and left Rome to find a place where he could serve God.

Taking with him his childhood nurse, who insisted on staying with him, he went to a place called Enside, east of Rome, and lived in a church there with some other godly men. Desiring solitude, he later went north to a cave at a place called Subiaco and lived in solitude for three years, fed by a friendly monk who discovered him there.

Even in this remote place, Benedict's reputation for godliness spread, and people sought him out. At the end of three years, the monks at a nearby monastery whose abbot (leader) had died begged Benedict to come and take the position of abbot. After much begging, Benedict consented. These men, however, were not godly, and objected to Benedict's attempts to bring order to the monastery. After they attempted to poison him, Benedict left for wilderness solitude once again.

After begging him to be their abbot, some monks rewarded Benedict's efforts by trying to poison him.

Some men more serious about living godly lives were still attracted to Benedict, and he was eventually able to establish twelve monasteries of twelve monks each. Here, too, tormented by a jealous local priest who tried to poison him,

Psalm Singing in the Monastery

"Above all else we urge that if anyone finds this distribution of the psalms unsatisfactory, he should arrange whatever he judges better, provided that the full complement of one hundred and fifty psalms is by all means carefully maintained every week, and that the series begins anew each Sunday at Vigils. For monks who in a week's time say less than the full psalter with the customary canticles betray extreme indolence and lack of devotion in their service. We read, after all, that our holy Fathers, energetic as they were, did all this in a single day. Let us hope that we, lukewarm as we are, can achieve it in a whole week . . .

"Let us consider, then, how we ought to behave in the presence of God and his angels, and let us stand to sing the psalms in such a way that our minds are in harmony with our voices."

Rule of St. Benedict, 18:22-25; 19:6-7; translation from Timothy Fry, editor, *RB 1980: The Rule of St. Benedict in English*, 1982, The Liturgical Press, p. 47.

Benedict was forced to leave and resettle with a few of his monks at Monte Cassino, southeast of Rome. Here he spent the rest of his life and, drawing on earlier monastic literature, wrote his famous *Rule* for monks. This was a guidebook on the spiritual and practical aspects of running a monastery. Benedict believed in community, humility, obedience to Jesus Christ, and imitating His life. He exhorted his monks to nonresistance, nonswearing of oaths, and repeatedly emphasized that grumbling should be avoided. He encouraged his monks to read, write, and employ themselves in manual labor. Benedict wrote:

Spiritual Teaching from St. Benedict

First of all, love the Lord God with your whole heart, your whole soul and all your strength, and love your neighbor as yourself (Matt 22:37-39; Mark 12:30-31; Luke 10:27) . . . Renounce yourself in order to follow Christ (Matt 16:24; Luke 9:23); discipline your body (1 Cor 9:27); do not pamper yourself, but love fasting. You must relieve the lot of the poor, clothe the naked, visit the sick (Matt 25:36), and bury the dead. Go to help the troubled and console the sorrowing.

Your way of acting should be different from the world's way; the love of Christ must come before all else. You are not to act in anger or nurse a grudge. Rid your heart of all deceit. Never give a hollow greeting of peace or turn away when someone needs your love. Bind yourself to no oath lest it prove false, but speak the truth with heart and tongue.

Do not repay one bad turn with another (1 Thess 5:15; 1 Pet 3:9). Do not injure anyone, but bear injuries patiently. Love your enemies (Matt 5:44; Luke 6:27). If people curse you, do not curse them back but bless them instead. Endure persecution for the sake of justice (Matt 5:10).

You must not be proud, nor be given to wine (Titus 1:7; 1 Tim 3:3). Refrain from too much eating or sleeping, and from laziness (Rom 12:11). Do not grumble or speak ill of others.

Place your hope in God alone. If you notice something good in yourself, give credit to God, not to yourself, but be certain that the evil you commit is always your own and yours to acknowledge.

Live in fear of judgment day and have a great horror of hell. Yearn for everlasting life with holy desire. Day by day remind yourself that you are going to die. Hour by hour keep careful watch over all you do, aware that God's gaze is upon you, wherever you may be. As soon as wrongful thoughts come into your heart, dash them against Christ and disclose them to your spiritual father. Guard your lips from harmful or deceptive speech. Prefer moderation in speech and speak no foolish chatter, nothing just to provoke laughter; do not love immoderate or boisterous laughter.

Listen readily to holy reading, and devote yourself often to prayer. Every day with tears and sighs confess your past sins to God in prayer and change from these evil ways in the future.

Do not gratify the promptings of the flesh (Gal 5:16); hate the urgings of self-will . . .

Do not aspire to be called holy before you really are, but first be holy that you may more truly be called so. Live by God's commandments every day; treasure chastity, harbor neither hatred nor jealousy of anyone, and do nothing out of envy. Do not love quarreling; shun arrogance. Respect the elders and love the young. Pray for your enemies out of love for Christ. If you have a dispute with someone, make peace with him before the sun goes down.

And finally, never lose hope in God's mercy.

Rule of St. Benedict, 4.1-2, 10-60, 62-74; translation from Timothy Fry, editor, *RB 1980: The Rule of St. Benedict in English*, 1982, The Liturgical Press, pp. 27-29.

Benedict the Wonder-Worker

One day at Monte Cassino, the monks were working on building the monastery and went to pick up a stone which they intended to use. The stone proved immovable for two or three monks, so they called for more help. To their frustration, they still could not get the stone to budge. Sudden inspiration hit them—the Devil was sitting on the stone. Upon realizing this, they called for Benedict, who prayed and blessed the stone, making it possible for the monks to lift it so easily that it seemed nearly weightless.

So says Pope Gregory the Great, the first biographer of Benedict, and himself a Black ("Benedictine") monk. Gregory wrote only about fifty years after Benedict's death and claimed to have received the information for his biography from several people who had known Benedict personally. Modern historians believe Gregory's biography was basically reliable in its outline, but the Pope's point was not to give a detailed historical or intellectual biography of the Saint. He was far more interested in stories of wonders and miracles worked by Benedict, many of which—such as the story above—strike us today as quite unlikely. Possible? Of course. Likely? Certainly not.

Medieval biographers who wrote the *Lives* of famous saints strike the modern mind as being nearly as gullible—and perhaps intentionally fictitious—as their contemporaries, the collectors of "relics" of all descriptions. While the relic hunters collected the bones, hair, clothing, and other artifacts attributed to the saints, the writers collected (and possibly invented) stories about them, recording them in *hagiographies*—from *hagios*, saint, and *graphe*, writing. In these works, the saints hardly appear to be real people at all, but some sort of superhuman wonder workers not at all like us.

Gregory's biography of Benedict is probably much more reliable than some of the later unbelievable productions. The goal of the hagiographer was edification, which was often accomplished at the expense of real history. Today, the term "hagiography" is still applied to historical or biographical writing which makes the heroes of the past look like perfect men without fault or blemish.

The labor of obedience will bring you back to him from whom you had drifted through the sloth of disobedience. This message of mine is for you, then, if you are ready to give up your own will, once and for all, and armed with the strong and noble weapons of obedience to do battle for the true King, Christ the Lord.

First of all, every time you begin a good work, you must pray to him most earnestly to bring it to perfection. In his goodness, he has already counted us as his sons, and therefore we should never grieve him by our evil actions . . .

With this conclusion, the Lord waits for us daily to translate into action, as we should, his holy teachings . . . We must, then, prepare our hearts and bodies for the battle of holy obedience to his instructions. What is not possible to us by nature, let us ask the Lord to supply by the help of his grace . . . as we progress in this way of life and in faith, we shall run on the path of God's commandments, our hearts overflowing with the inexpressible delight of love. Never swerving from his instructions, then, but faithfully observing his teaching in the monastery until death, we shall through patience share in the sufferings of Christ that we may deserve also to share in his kingdom.[2]

Benedict's *Rule* eventually won a place of great respect among monks in the West, and centuries later, many European monks came to be called "Benedictines." Unfortunately, monasticism did not always remain a pure witness to Jesus' teachings and a more faithful form of Christianity. Acceptance from earthly rulers came at a price—monasteries were drawn into political involvements, compromising their dedication to a separated, spiritual life. Some rulers donated land to monasteries, ensuring that the monks would continually pray for them. In this way, the busy lord did not need to perform penance for all his sins, since he had monks to pray for him. In this way, instead of offering a prophetic dissent against worldly and violent ways, the monks' sanctity was called upon as a blessing to it—the "perfect" could pray for and procure forgiveness for the "imperfect" who chose to live a less-dedicated Christianity.

Later, lords who donated land to monasteries became titular abbots—having the title of abbot without actually being monks—with authority over the monasteries on their lands. This image of a secular abbot ruling over a monastery for his own personal gain was very different from Benedict's concept of the abbot chosen from among the monks to guide them in the ways of God.

As monasteries increased in land holdings, they came to fill the place of feudal lords for the peasants living on their lands (see sidebar on page 23). The peasants farmed the land for the monks, and the monastery collected the peasants' taxes and dues. Rather than monks working for their own living—as was Benedict's concept—monks collected their living from the work of the peasants, and the monastic litur-

---

2   *Rule of St. Benedict*, Prologue:2-5, 35, 40-41, 49-50; translation from Timothy Fry, editor, *RB 1980: The Rule of St. Benedict in English*, 1982, The Liturgical Press, pp. 15, 18-19.

Do Penance

While our English Bibles say that Jesus and John the Baptist exhorted their hearers to "repent," the Vulgate, the Latin Bible in use in Europe for centuries, has the phrase "do penance" in those verses. In Roman Catholic theology, penance is both a virtue and a sacrament. As a virtue, it is an attitude of repentance, consisting both of sorrow for sin and a determination not to repeat the offense.

As a sacrament, penance consists of confession, the penance itself (the acts of penance), and absolution (forgiveness).

Imagine for a moment that someone in your church has committed a serious sin, and the church wants to see evidence of repentance before reaccepting him as a member. What would you look for as evidence? Prayer? Fasting? Almsgiving? All three?

These were some of the evidences which the church, in its early centuries, looked for as evidences of repentance. Eventually, these acts began to be suggested or prescribed as what the fallen one had to do to be at peace with the church. In addition to prayer, fasting, and almsgiving, medieval practice included other acts which could serve as penance, including pilgrimages, venerating holy relics (the bones of saints), or even harming one's own body.

Such acts of penance were always supposed to be connected with an attitude of real repentance, and were to help the sinner hate his sin and strengthen his resolve to practice righteousness. However, in many people's minds, the acts of penance became mechanical. Penance became something done as satisfaction for their sins, rather than to show sincerity of repentance. Some reasoned that if the works of penance were done, they would have forgiveness, apart from the state of their hearts—that is, whether they were *repentant* or not. Thus, one could have princes who provided land for monks to live on and perform penance on his behalf, even though he had no intentions of stopping his sins, such as war or fornication.

gy grew until it took nearly the whole day to perform. While Benedict's monks lived lives of prayer, reading, and work, later monks did no work, little reading, and spent nearly all their time in performing church services.

Amid these changes, spiritual and even moral laxity set in. Some monks recognized this, and reforming orders such as the Cistercians were begun. Eventually, these orders also became wealthy and drifted from the visions of their founders.

Michael Sattler

Monasticism forms the background for the story of Michael Sattler. As a young man, he joined the Benedictine monastery of St. Peter's in the Black Forest. We unfortunately know little of Michael Sattler's early life. He was born in the small German town of Stauffen im Breisgau, located in the lower Black Forest in southwest Germany. Some background information on St. Peter's will help us understand Michael Sattler's story.

A traditional Black Forest farmhouse. Michael Sattler may have spent his boyhood in a house much like this one.

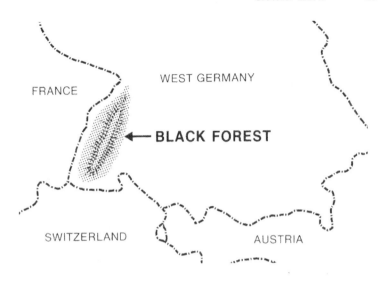

St. Peter's of the Black Forest was founded by a noble family in 1073. At the time, many Benedictine monasteries were trying to reform the relationships between themselves and the system which allowed secular "abbots" to rule over them. The compromise reached involved monasteries being allowed to freely elect their own abbots, but each monastery would also have a secular overseer who would be the legal advocate for the monastery and would oversee the monastic property. The monastery elected the overseer, but the overseer could only be elected from among the descendants of the founding family.

St. Peter's was founded with this arrangement, and it prospered until 1238, when a fire destroyed the monastery. Although it was rebuilt in 1275, catastrophes of famine, plague, war, and oppressive overseers kept the monastery in a state of financial difficulty for centuries.

In 1437, St. Peter's burned to the ground once again, and the monastery was in a financially perilous state. No major rebuilding occurred until around 1496, about the time Michael Sattler was born. Thus, as a young man, he joined a monastery quite strapped for cash, poorer than other near-

The façade of the St. Peter's monastery church as it appears today. It has been rebuilt since Michael Sattler's time.

by monasteries, and in debt due to the building of its new church, which was dedicated in 1500.

Jodocus Kaiser was elected abbot of the monastery in 1512; whether Michael was already a monk, we do not know. We do know that Kaiser was Michael's abbot and that Michael left the monastery while Kaiser was still abbot. After Michael joined the monastery, it continued to have financial troubles. The Reformation, beginning in 1517, did not at first impact the monastery much, and did not gain a sympathetic ear there. The monastery's annals record:

in the year 1517, in which Martin Luther began to spread his teachings, there was an enormous shortage of crops lasting the entire year. . . . Earthquakes were felt in many places with enormous injury. For many people the earthquakes were followed by a mortal illness of the head and the destruction of the mind.[3]

Despite rejecting the Protestant Reformation, Abbot Jodocus was interested in another reform movement among the Benedictine Order, attempting to return monasteries to a purer observance of the Rule of St. Benedict. Jodocus began the process of initiating such a reform at St. Peter's.

Perhaps Michael's seriousness about the Christian life and/or his leadership abilities were evident even in his monastery days; perhaps this seriousness manifested itself in his being in favor of reforming the monastery. We do not know. In any case, sometime after 1518, he was appointed as the prior of the monastery—the second position of authority under the abbot. He had become a "cloister lord" and a leader of men.

---

3   C. Arnold Snyder, *The Life and Thought of Michael Sattler*, © 1984, Herald Press (Scottdale, PA 15683), p. 41. Used by permission.

Beat Your Plowshares into Swords

But Michael's peaceful monastery days were not to last forever. He began studying the epistles of Paul, and saw that he was in an "unchristian and dangerous estate."[4] The pomp and pride of the Roman Catholic Church and of monastery life became evident to him. The immorality of the supposedly "perfect" monks and priests brought him closer to the decision to leave the monastery. He also became disturbed by the system's usury.

St. Peter's had significant land holdings and was a feudal lord over the peasants living on its lands, collecting taxes and rents from them. Due to the debt the monastery had incurred from its building projects and general inflation, St. Peter's continued to be in financial straits. The peasants' rents were fixed, however; the monastery could not adjust them upward because of inflation. Abbot Jodocus became stricter in enforcing the rents and payments, and the peasants complained that their rights were being ignored. Then, in 1519, the Austrian government imposed a new tax on its subjects (including monasteries), and Jodocus simply taxed the peasants more to pay the monastery's tax. The peasants refused to pay and complained, but found no sympathy from the Abbot.

Abbot Jodocus called on the monastery's overseer, Margrave Ernst of Hachberg, to enforce the monastery's rights against its peasant serfs. The overseer did not act on the monastery's behalf, and the Abbot then appealed to the Austrian government. The peasants complained to Margrave Ernst and found in him a listening ear. Ernst gathered his army of mercenaries and invaded the monastery. Abbot Jodocus fled to the protection of the nearby city of Freiburg.

---

4   This is what he told the court in his trial. John Howard Yoder, translator and editor, *The Legacy of Michael Sattler*, © 1973, Herald Press (Scottdale, PA 15683), p. 72. Used by permission.

Feudalism

Feudalism was the social, governmental, and economic system which prevailed in Europe during the Middle Ages.

The structure was based on the relationship between a lord and his vassals. In exchange for military, financial, and other services, a lord would grant land to his vassals (subjects who entered into this feudal relationship with an overlord). These vassals could, in turn, subdivide the land and grant parts of it to others, who would become their vassals. Thus, the middle grade was, at the same time, both lords and vassals. At the top was the king or emperor; at the bottom was the serf or peasant.

The serf or peasant was allowed to live on and farm the land held by the lord of the manor. In return, the peasant gave the lord a portion of the proceeds as well as farming the lord's own farmland. The peasant was not allowed to move to another manor; he was "bound to the land."

By the time of the Reformation, feudalism was beginning to crumble. The rise of towns gave rise to classes of merchants and artisans who did not farm the land or work for a feudal lord. This accelerated the rise of a money economy, in which land was not the only or necessarily the most valuable form of wealth. Out of this new situation, capitalism—where capital (the means of production, including land) was privately owned and used for profit—arose.

Abbot Jodocus wrote to the prior (who at this time was probably Sattler) with instructions not to give food or drink to the invading army. So the mercenaries took the monastery's keys themselves, but after explaining to the monks why they were invading, the monks agreed to feed them.

Serfs had to work hard to pay their taxes and dues to the lords and their tithes to the church. Hopefully something would be left over for them and their families to eat!

With the monastery occupied by mercenaries under the command of the monastery's own overseer, there was no way Prior Michael Sattler could have escaped wrestling with the implications of the "perfect" monks making a living off of the labors of others. The subjects of monasteries were often under heavier economic burdens than their neighbors under secular landlords, and monastic landlords felt free to threat-

The Tithe

Today, "tithing" means voluntarily dropping a check in the offering plate at church for 10% of your income that week. For peasants in the Middle Ages, tithing was not voluntary—it was a government-enforced church tax.

All week long, the peasant worked hard, and much of the fruit of his labor went to the lord of the manor. Then, he went to church, and was required to "donate" 10% of his remaining income to the church.

It might not have been so bad if the money had gone to support the local priest who cared for the donating peasant. But too often, it did not. The tithe often went to pay absentee clergy who rarely visited the parish. Some of these clergy received pay from multiple parishes. The higher up the ecclesiastical ladder, the richer the bishop or archbishop probably was, and the less need he had of the peasants' money.

This was enough to make the peasants upset about the tithe. But now imagine that your feudal lord was a monastery, and much of the fruit of your labor went—in taxes and dues—to the monks, who did not work to support themselves. Then you went to church and paid your tithe, but that tithe was owned by the monastery—and that 10% also went straight to the monks.

Is it any wonder that the peasants found this system profoundly frustrating and unchristian?

en peasants with excommunication to collect overdue money. In addition, many of the churches in the area were under the control of monasteries (including St. Peter's), meaning that the tithe money for the church went, not to support the priests who directly served the people paying the tithe, but to the monastery. This complex tangle of politics and money—all oppressing the peasants—probably came to be viewed by

Michael Sattler as "usury," and became one of the reasons he left the monastery.[5]

The invasion of the monastery provoked the anger of the Freiburg senate and the local Austrian government. Margrave Ernst withdrew his army from the monastery, and the next year offered to sell his overseership to Archduke Ferdinand of Austria for 1,000 gulden—a sum which the monastery would have to repay to the archduke later. Not long after, the Peasant's War broke out, and the peasant subjects of St. Peter's monastery participated.

The lot of the peasants in medieval Europe had grown progressively worse through the centuries. Traditional rights and privileges had been slowly and steadily taken away by their feudal lords. Feeling oppressed and trapped in cycles of poverty, the peasants wished to be free. Reformation preaching added fuel to the fire. Across the German lands, people were being told that the Roman Catholic Church was committing unchristian abominations, that the pope was the antichrist, and Catholic ceremonies were superstitious sins. Yet actually stopping the saying of the Mass, removing the images from churches, or removing from their offices priests who refused to preach the Word of God, was not allowed. Furthermore, the reform-minded preachers were sometimes persecuted by the authorities. This frustrated many of the common people.

The Peasants' War began in late May 1524, when the subjects of the Abbey of St. Blasien, southeast of St. Peter's, rebelled, refusing to render feudal dues and services. Through the rest of 1524, peasant unrest and rebellion spread rapidly throughout the Black Forest and Upper Swabia. Rebellion mostly took the form of strikes and protests, and peasants gathered in huge bands and forced their overlords to nego-

---

5   In his trial, Sattler mentioned "usury," along with the immorality of priests and monks, as one of the reasons he left the monastery. John Howard Yoder, *The Legacy of Michael Sattler*, 1973, Herald Press, p. 72.

The Demands of the Peasants

The peasants wrote a list of their goals, called *The Twelve Articles of the Peasants*. These goals are summarized below. Note that the first two were fulfilled in the Anabaptist movement.

1. Each community should have the right to choose its own pastor and depose him in the case of wrongdoing.
2. Tithes should be spent first for the support of the pastor, second for the support of the poor within the community, and if any is left over, it should be saved for use within the community.
3. The end of serfdom, as all men should be free.
4. Peasants should have hunting and fishing rights.
5. Forests should be freely used for the good of the whole community.
6. Forced work days for the lords should be reduced.
7. Peasants should be paid when they work for the lords.
8. Rents should be adjusted.
9. The constant making of new laws should be stopped.
10. Meadows and fields formerly owned by communities should revert to the use of those communities, rather than of the lords who had appropriated them.
11. The inheritance tax should be repealed.
12. All of these articles should be examined by the Word of God; any found to be inconsistent with it would be retracted.

tiate. The movement was basically nonviolent at this stage. Nevertheless, negotiations failed to settle the differences between the peasants and their lords, and in early 1525, the movement developed further.

In early 1525, the peasants began broadly appealing to "the Word of God" as justification for their demands, and two sympathetic preachers compiled the peasants' grievances into the Twelve Articles, which became a definitive and versatile statement of peasant demands during the revolt.

The coat of arms of St. Peter's of the Black Forest.

In mid-April, the peasants in the Black Forest revolted afresh, and this time the rebellion turned violent. They embarked on a military campaign until mid-June, attacking towns and seeking to force them to submit to peasant demands and join the peasant bands. The height of their success came on May 23, 1525.

Prior to this, the peasants ruled by Margrave Ernst rebelled against him, and successfully took over his castles. Ernst fled to Freiburg for his safety. The peasants south of Freiburg rebelled as well, and by May 12, the city was completely besieged. Abbot Jodocus also fled to Freiburg, and St. Peter's Monastery was occupied by rebelling peasants on May 12. Was Sattler still there? If so, he once again had to negotiate with rebellious peasants, who did not burn or plunder the monastery.

The peasants began negotiating with the city, writing that "They were burdened with taxes to such an extent that they could no longer bear it. They demanded first of all that the Word of God be purely proclaimed to the common man.

St. Peter's of the Black Forest as it appears today.

What the holy gospel allowed they wished to leave to the [discretion of the] clergy and worldly magistracy."[6] Freiburg refused to surrender, and prepared itself for battle. A few skirmishes resulted in peasant victories, and the city, realizing that it was outnumbered, disadvantaged, and had limited water, finally surrendered to the peasants on May 23, 1525.

This was the height of peasant success in the Black Forest. The next day, the fortress of Breisach surrendered to the peasants. They then marched southeast and besieged Radolfzell, this time without success. As the lords' soldiers of the Swabian League began to win victories over the peasants, the peasants and the lords finally made peace. This brought the Peasants' War in the Black Forest to an end.

If Michael Sattler was still the prior at St. Peter's at this time, he would have had to negotiate with the rebels who occupied the monastery. It may have been his first contact

---

6   C. Arnold Snyder, *The Life and Thought of Michael Sattler*, © 1984, Herald Press (Scottdale, PA 15683), p. 61. Used by permission.

with Anabaptists, for the troop of peasants which occupied the monastery included Anabaptist volunteers from the cities of Waldshut and Hallau. When did Michael Sattler depart the monastery? What did he do when he left? We do not know the answers to these questions; evidence is lacking. We know that he did leave the monastery, probably in the early 1520s, and arrived in Zürich, Switzerland, sometime in 1525. When he left the monastery, he rejected forever the pride, immorality, and usury that he had found among the monks.

Margaretha

> When God called me to testify to His Word, and I read Paul, I considered the unchristian and dangerous estate in which I had been, in view of the pomp, pride, usury, and great fornication of the monks and priests. I therefore obeyed and took a wife according to the command of God.[7]
>
> —*Michael Sattler*

Sometime after leaving the monastery, Michael married a beautiful and intelligent woman by the name of Margaretha, who had previously been a Beguine. The Beguines were a semi-monastic organization for women. Beguines were not nuns, nor did they take life-long vows, as did regular orders of monks and nuns. Beguines were free to leave the organization and marry whenever they wished. Some Beguines lived in their own homes or even with their families; some would buy houses and live together. Others would build large complexes in which to live, often in or near cities and similar to monasteries. Each home within the complex, however, was privately owned by individual Beguines. The Beguines op-

---

7   John Howard Yoder, translator and editor, *The Legacy of Michael Sattler*, © 1973, Herald Press (Scottdale, PA 15683), p. 72. Used by permission.

Anabaptist Peasant Rebels?

Balthasar Hubmaier was Anabaptism's only degreed theologian. His book *On the Christian Baptism of Believers*, published in July 1525, is often said to be one of the best written defenses of believers' baptism. It certainly was when it was published.

Hubmaier was a friend of Conrad Grebel and several other Swiss Anabaptists. He had been a Zwinglian reformer in the city of Waldshut in Austria, but through his own studies of the Scriptures and through Anabaptist influence, he came to reject infant baptism and he and nearly the whole town were rebaptized in the spring of 1525.

Despite now being an "Anabaptist," Hubmaier never embraced nonresistance, nor did he reject the state church concept. In 1524, as the Catholic Austrian government was furious at the Protestant city, Waldshut made a defensive alliance with the rebelling peasants, and it participated in the rebellion despite many of its citizens being rebaptized in 1525.

Hubmaier approved of the *Twelve Articles*, and some "Anabaptists" from Waldshut joined the rebelling peasants. Hubmaier escaped the city just before it fell to Austrian troops, who forcibly restored Catholic worship in the city.

Hubmaier eventually made his way to Moravia, where in Nikolsburg he again tried to establish an Anabaptist state church. His final published writing was a book arguing against nonresistance. A few weeks after its publication, he was arrested and later burned at the stake by the Austrians for his crimes of rebaptism and inciting rebellion.

Two of Michael Sattler's Anabaptist friends were Ulrich Teck and Jacob Gross. These two men had been expelled from "Anabaptist" Waldshut for refusing to bear arms in the city's defense.

erated businesses and practiced trades; however, their main focus was ministry. They would care for the ill (particularly lepers) and dying; help prostitutes to escape their sinful

Many Beguines poured out their lives to help others, both physically and spiritually.

lifestyles; teach children; and help the poor and women prisoners. They often had a concern for church reform and stood against the moral and spiritual laxity of their time. Due to this, they would sometimes preach in public places, exhorting people to repentance, and even sometimes translated the Scriptures into the vernacular languages. They were often suspected of heresy, and some were even executed.

With this background, it is not surprising that an ex-Beguine would be attracted to a young man like Michael Sattler—serious and spiritual, an ex-Benedictine repulsed by the carnality of the monks, hoping to reform the church. The two seem to have made an excellent match.

But the time would come [when] God would so arrange [matters] and grant grace to man in order to let himself baptize.

~Attributed to Michael Sattler

3

In Search of Grace

Jn the mid-1520s, having left the monastery and possibly already married, Michael Sattler went to Zürich. We do not know what attracted him to the city. He showed up while controversy raged between the official, state church reformers—Ulrich Zwingli and his colleagues—and the Anabaptists. He may have attended the second disputation on baptism, November 6-8, 1525. He must have shown enough interest in Anabaptism to get himself arrested by the Zürich government, and in the aftermath of the November disputation, he was put on trial with the rest of the Anabaptist prisoners. He was not himself an Anabaptist at that time, and was probably not convinced of the truth of the Anabaptist teaching on baptism. He swore an oath of loyalty to the Zürich government, paid the costs of his imprisonment, and was released.

On the same occasion, Conrad Grebel, Felix Mantz, and George Blaurock were sentenced to imprisonment on a diet of bread, mush, and water. Did Michael Sattler have the

The early Anabaptists had to meet in hiding to avoid capture by their persecutors. This cave in Switzerland, now known as the Täuferhöhle (Anabaptist cave) is one location where they met.

opportunity, before their imprisonment, to spend time with these three men and learn from them? While we may never know for sure, it seems likely that Michael did have at least some personal contact with them and learned from them.

Following this experience, Michael did not lose his interest in Anabaptism. He may have moved into the home of Hans Kuenzi, a former Anabaptist, to learn the weaver's trade. Like many other ex-monks during Reformation times, Michael probably wanted to follow the example of the Apostle Paul and support himself with honest labor.

Hans Kuenzi wrote a letter to the Zürich authorities around May 1526, requesting that they would allow him to return to his home, which he had fled to avoid arrest. We know from the letter that a former monk by the name of Michael was living in his home—possibly Michael Sattler.[1]

---

1   However, a convincing case has also been made that it was Michael Wüst,

A weaver at his loom in the 1500s.

Further, a person came to me who had also been a monk, who urged me for the sake of love to teach him to work, for he wished to eat bread from his own hand, in humility, which I desired to do for him following the command of God; by this it is assumed that he is the same Michael who earlier had also been your prisoner. But this is not true. Therefore, you have pressed me the more decidedly. And this same [person] has conducted himself around us in a quiet manner and has not dealt with baptism and also is not [re]baptized. In addition, he went once with my brother . . . at my suggestion on account of a young woman, where he was asked to read [to the group], and where there was quite a crowd present.[2]

This letter references two Michaels, one who had been a prisoner in Zürich, the other who had been a guest of Kuenzi's. Since Michael Wüst may also have spent time in prison

another early Swiss Anabaptist. See Heinold Fast, "Michael Sattler's Baptism: Some Comments," *Mennonite Quarterly Review* 60(3) (July 1986):364-373; see also Arnold Snyder, "Michael Sattler's Baptism: Some Comments in Reply to Heinold Fast," *Mennonite Quarterly Review* 62(4) (October 1988):496-506.
2   Translation compiled from C. Arnold Snyder, *The Life and Thought of Michael Sattler*, © 1984, Herald Press (Scottdale, PA 15683), p. 83 (used by permission), and Heinold Fast, "Michael Sattler's Baptism: Some Comments," *Mennonite Quarterly Review* 60(3) (July 1986):364-373, p. 369.

The Historian's Trade

Imagine you are writing a letter to a friend about another person, discussing a situation or set of circumstances with which you are both familiar. There is no need to explain the background in depth; you both know that. Suppose further that you are afraid your friend's children or little siblings might see the letter, and so you decide to write in a rather cryptic fashion—saying what is necessary so that you and the intended recipient know what is being communicated, but others will have difficulty understanding.

Now suppose that the subject of your letter, in two or three hundred years, has become famous, and historians are looking high and low for information to fill in this person's biography. One historian finds your letter, publishes it in a historical journal, and an intense scholarly debate ensues about exactly what you were trying to say, and even whether you were talking about the famous person or not. Some take one side, some another, but your cryptic message was not written with history in mind; it was written to communicate information to one person—your friend—and no other.

This is the kind of situation historians find themselves in—debating possible interpretations of sources which are unclear, and which were not written with history in mind. It is fair to assume that the Zürich government officials knew what Hans Kuenzi meant when he spoke about the "person . . . who had also been a monk." But unless another letter is found which clarifies the meaning, we may be left forever in the dark, limited to making educated guesses about who Hans was referring to.

in Zürich, in addition to Michael Sattler, identification of the letter's subject is almost impossible. Assuming that Kuenzi's guest was Michael Sattler, we can conclude that he was not yet baptized as of May 1526, and was in Hans Kuenzi's home learning to weave. At this point in his life, he was not outwardly very interested in Anabaptism—he was now only minimally involved with the Anabaptists, having attended a meeting as a reader.

In July 1526, Annli Fürstin and her husband, Hans Nessler, gave court testimony about their contacts with Anabaptists. They seem to have met Michael Sattler sometime before or soon after Hans Kuenzi's letter had been written. In Annli's testimony, Michael appears again as not fully committed to the cross of baptism. She told the court:

> It was true that Oggenfuss [another Anabaptist], a tailor in Seeb, had been with them, and, yes, someone from Stouffen at Kimenhof [Michael Sattler]. But had not discussed baptism but only said that it was not necessary to be baptized: but the time would come [when] God would so arrange [matters] and grant grace to man in order to let himself baptize.[3]

Sometime after this, Michael Sattler was baptized and joined the persecuted Swiss Brethren. We do not know exactly when, where, or by whom he was baptized, but once he was committed, he became a powerful builder of the Kingdom of God.

---

3   Heinold Fast, "Michael Sattler's Baptism: Some Comments," *Mennonite Quarterly Review* 60(3) (July 1986):364-373, p. 373.

Going to Church with 1520s Anabaptists

Early Swiss Brethren meetings were basically home Bible studies. The leader of the meeting was the "reader," who would read the Scripture passage to be discussed and would moderate the discussion. When arrested and questioned, these "readers" would often argue that they did not "teach" or "preach," but only "read." (Unauthorized "preaching" carried stiffer penalties.)

The Swiss Congregational Order, the oldest Anabaptist *Ordnung*, was probably written by this time and gives us some insight into what these meetings were like. Article 1 says: "To meet at least three or four times a week, to exercise ourselves in the teaching of Christ and his apostles, to admonish and encourage one another from the heart to remain faithful to Jesus as we have promised." Article 2 describes the meeting itself: "When the brothers and sisters meet, they shall choose a Scripture to read together. The one to whom God has given the best understanding shall explain it, the others should be still and listen, so that there are not two or three carrying on a private conversation, bothering the others." These meetings then closed with the observance of Communion, described in Article 7: "Every time the believers meet for worship, they should break bread and drink wine to proclaim the death of the Lord. Everyone should remember, through this, how Christ gave his life for us, how his blood was poured out for us, so we may become willing to give our bodies and lives to Christ—that is to all our brothers and sisters in him."

If Hans Kuenzi's letter is indeed describing Michael Sattler, then he had his first Anabaptist ministry experience as a "reader" in meetings like this.

"He demonstrated at all times an excellent zeal for the honor of God and the church of Christ, which he desired to see righteous and honorable, free of vices, irreproachable, and to be by their righteous life a help to those who are without."

~ Wolfgang Capito, describing Michael Sattler

4
Evangelist and Ambassador

By June, 1526, Michael Sattler was north of Zürich, working with several others, evangelizing and baptizing. In late December 1526/January 1527, he turned his steps toward the German city of Strasbourg (now in France), where he interacted with the Zwinglian reformers there: Martin Bucer and Wolfgang Capito.

Strasbourg was a Free Imperial City, meaning that it was directly under the authority of the emperor and not answerable to lower lords. It was ruled by a City Council rather than an overlord. Thus, it had considerably more freedom over its own affairs than other cities under the rule of the lords. In Strasbourg's case, with a Burgomeister (mayor) in favor of the Reformation, this freedom manifested itself in religious reform and greater religious toleration than in many of the other cities in the Holy Roman Empire.

Martin Bucer and Wolfgang Capito were the main reformation preachers in the city. They were friends of Ulrich

Zwingli in Zürich, but had more sympathy with Anabaptists than he did. Bucer and Capito did not agree with Zwingli's fierce and violent repression of the Anabaptist movement, and while Strasbourg did not tolerate Anabaptists, it never sentenced one to death.

Anabaptism came to the city of Strasbourg in 1525. In 1526, Wilhelm Reublin arrived, and opposition to infant baptism in the city increased. Later in the year, Anabaptist leaders Hans Denck, Jacob Gross, and Michael Sattler arrived.

Prior to Sattler's arrival, Bucer and Capito had first a private, then a public disputation with Hans Denck. Denck had accepted believers' baptism, but was a spiritualist Anabaptist—he minimized the importance of outward ordinances like baptism and the Lord's Supper and emphasized the inner realities they represented. This led him, by the end of his life, to repudiate his participation in baptizing others. He was accused of accepting universalism (that all would eventually be saved) and other views disturbing to the reformation preachers. Following the disputations, Denck was banished from Strasbourg, and soon after, several other Anabaptists, including Sattler's friend Jacob Gross, were arrested and imprisoned.

Sattler seems to have heard of the imprisonment of his brethren and particularly of his friend and co-laborer Gross. He made his way to Strasbourg to plead with the preachers for mercy for his friends. As far as we know, he did not evangelize or baptize in the city, but devoted his time to discussions with Bucer and Capito.

The two reformers—particularly Capito—found in Sattler someone they could appreciate. "He demonstrated at all times an excellent zeal for the honor of God and the church of Christ, which he desired to see righteous and honorable, free of vices, irreproachable, and to be by their righteous life a help to those who are without," Capito later wrote.

The Holy Roman Empire of the German Nation

In the sixteenth century, there was no such country as "Germany." The term "Germany," in speaking of that time, is used in a general way of the German-speaking lands which later made up the modern-day nation of Germany. These lands were a patchwork of tiny states and independent cities, ruled by princes, dukes, city councils, or even bishops. The patchwork was constantly shifting and changing, as these states were often at odds—and sometimes war—with each other.

In theory, the Germans were bound together as the "Holy Roman Empire," which saw itself as the continuation or successor of the Roman Empire, and its emperors as the successors of the Roman emperors.

The emperor ruled for life, and upon his decease, seven German rulers known as electors chose his successor. While it was somewhat democratic, from 1437 on, the Holy Roman Emperor was (with one three-year exception) always chosen from the Habsburg family.

Although in theory the emperor was ruler over the Germans, he actually needed to keep the electors happy. If the emperor wanted to make war, he needed the electors to cooperate, as they held the real authority over the people and materials of the empire.

The Holy Roman Empire survived until 1806, when Napoleon brought it to an end.

The city of Strasbourg, where Michael Sattler asked the reformers for mercy on his Anabaptist friends in prison there.

"This intention we never reprimanded but rather praised and encouraged."[1] Sattler tried to convince them of the validity of a pure church, separated from the world and its wickedness, entered into by a voluntary commitment in believers' baptism and kept pure by church discipline. To the reformers, this sounded like legalism. To Sattler, the corrupt life of the state church made it unthinkable that its preachers could possibly be right. Capito wrote, "But since besides in addition to our faithful teaching and that of other preachers there may well be shortcomings among the people who claim to be Christian, a life found to be offensive, it was for this reason, if I understand, that he took so little to heart what we basically argued to clarify the truth."[2] In response to all his pleas for obedience to the words of Scripture with regards to baptism, nonresistance, and separation from the world, the

---

1   John Howard Yoder, translator and editor, *The Legacy of Michael Sattler*, © 1973, Herald Press (Scottdale, PA 15683), p. 87. Used by permission.
2   *Ibid.*

On the right and in the distance can be seen the Strasbourg cathedral, its single spire soaring into the sky.

Strasbourg reformers argued that since love is the end of the law (I Timothy 1:5), thus "love" must govern all things and all observance of Scriptural commands. By this they meant that if some were yet offended by discontinuing infant baptism, infant baptism should be continued for the sake of "love." It was a similar concept to Zwingli's "forbearance" for the sake of "the weak."

Sattler could not accept such a plea. He saw in the Scriptures that believers are to be Christ-like; thus, what He did and commanded, they should also do. God's kingdom is in opposition to the kingdom of the world and the devil; the two are separate and can have nothing to do with each other. Thus, to follow Christ in nonresistance, for example, is not something *optional*; the members of Christ's body *must* be minded as the Head, Christ, is.

Sattler devoted some time to these discussions with the Protestant reformers in the city of Strasbourg, each side trying to convince the other. Only a few months after his

The Strasbourg Cathedral.

baptism, Sattler had already become a skilled and articulate defender of Anabaptist beliefs. No doubt, Bucer and Capito would have loved to convince Michael Sattler to join their own cause and help in the official reformation in Strasbourg, but trying to live a godly life in the midst of an ungodly state church did not line up with what Michael Sattler and his brothers and sisters had understood from the Scriptures. The day finally came when Michael realized he had to leave Strasbourg, as he was getting nowhere with the reformers.

Having come to this realization, Michael took pen in hand and wrote a farewell letter to his friends—the first surviving writing we have from his hand.

> Michael Sattler to his beloved brothers in God Capito and Bucer and others who love and confess Christ from the heart.

Grace and peace from God our Father through Jesus
Christ our Savior. Dear brothers in God! As I recently
spoke with you in brotherly moderation and friendliness
on several points, which I together with my brothers and
sisters have understood out of Scripture, namely out of
the New Testament, and you for your part as the ones
asked answered in similar moderation and friendliness . . . [3]

Michael gave twenty one-line reasons which "hinder me,
dear brothers, from understanding your general assertion on
every subject which you advocate with the words of Paul
cited above," referring to their use of I Timothy 1:5. Beginning with how faith in Christ reconciles us with God and
gives access to Him, Sattler puts forward baptism as the act
which incorporates believers into Christ's body, the church,
of which He is the Head. The members of this church must
be minded as the Head is minded, and conformed to His image. The world, under the rule of the devil, is against the
kingdom of Christ, and its citizens hate Christ's citizens.
Christians are those who have *gelassenheit*, full submission
and yieldedness to God; thus, they trust Him rather than
physical weapons. True Christians, Sattler says, are those
"who practice in deed the teaching of Christ." The world
cannot comprehend the kingdom of Christ; "There is nothing in common between Christ and Belial."[4]

The two kingdom concept, and the separation of these
two kingdoms from each other, comes out in this letter as
central to Sattler's thought. The kingdom of Christ is defined by faith, yieldedness (*gelassenheit*), and a growing
into Christlikeness and obedience to Christ's teachings. The
devil's kingdom, on the other hand, is defined by darkness,
force, persecution, destruction, and a lack of comprehension
of Christ's kingdom.

---

3   John Howard Yoder, translator and editor, *The Legacy of Michael Sattler*,
© 1973, Herald Press (Scottdale, PA 15683), p. 21-22. Used by permission.
4   *Ibid.*

Gelassenheit

Gelassenheit was an essential early Anabaptist concept. Gelassenheit is a German word which has no exact English translation which captures its full essence. Anabaptist historian Robert Friedmann wrote that gelassenheit was "self-surrender, resignation in God's will . . . yieldedness to God's will, self-abandonment, the (passive) opening to God's willing, including the readiness to suffer for the sake of God, also peace and calmness of mind."[1]

Early Anabaptists were not the first to use the gelassenheit concept. In the Middle Ages, the mystics used the term often. Mystics were Catholics who sought for a true, inner spiritual life, rather than a focus on sacraments while living an ungodly life. Mystical works such as the *Theologia Germanica* influenced the later Anabaptists.

To mystics, gelassenheit was primarily *inner detachment*. The heart's attachment to created things was evil unbelief, out of which grew selfishness and sin. The man who is *gelassen* is "detached" in his heart from all earthly possessions, and reliant on God alone. He finds his satisfaction and fulfillment in his relationship with God, not in possessing or using earthly things.

To this, the early Anabaptists added the concept of gelassenheit as full surrender and acceptance of God's will, particularly suffering for the sake of righteousness. This is not the gloomy fatalism of the pessimist; it is rather a posture of delighting to do God's will (Psalm 40:8). It is a determination that no matter what opposition one may encounter from the world, the devil, and one's own flesh and desires, the disciple will persevere in doing God's will rather than his own.

---

1   Robert Friedmann, "Gelassenheit," *in* Harold S. Bender, Cornelius Krahn, & Melvin Gingerich (editors), *The Mennonite Encyclopedia*, Volume II, © 1956, Mennonite Publishing House (Scottdale, PA 15683), p. 448. Used by permission.

An anonymous Swiss Anabaptist explains the connection between gelassenheit and being part of the true church through baptism and the Lord's Supper.

> So by now the Christian life should be clearly visible to all Christians: all Christ's teaching is the Christians' teaching; his love, our love; his mercy, our mercy; his patience, our patience; his peace, our peace; his suffering, our suffering; his death, our death; his resurrection, our resurrection; his ascension, our ascension . . . Therefore, whoever surrenders to such a Christian life may be baptized in the name of Christ, and partake of the Holy Supper with all true Christians . . . Such must first surrender to Christ in faith and trust, and allow themselves to be purified by [Christ], and surrender unto His true obedience, on the basis of which they may be baptized properly . . .'

2   Anonymous Swiss Anabaptists, *A Short, Simple Confession*, 1580s; translation from C. Arnold Snyder (editor), *Later Writings of the Swiss Anabaptists 1529-1592*, 2017, Pandora Press, pp. 208-209.

"Herewith I commend you to the Lord, for as I understand it, I can no longer remain here without doing a special dishonor to God; therefore I must for the sake of my conscience leave the field to the opposition. I beg you herein, that you understand this as an act of Christian humility on my part. The Lord will ultimately dispose,"[5] Sattler wrote.

He closed with a final plea for his friends in prison and for religious freedom.

> Be mercifully considerate, I pray you, of those who are in prison and do not permit a merciful judgment to be superseded by a blind, spiteful, and cruel one. Those

5   *Ibid.*

Michael Sattler's letter to the reformers in his own handwriting.

who are in error (if that they were) are not to be coerced but after a second admonition to be avoided. Christians admonish benevolently, out of sympathy and compassion for the sinful, and do not legalistically coerce persons this way or that.[6]

With that, Sattler left Strasbourg and appears to have gone to nearby Lahr. Jacob Gross was banished from Strasbourg. (The full text of Michael's letter to the reformers is on page 109.)

Lahr

Jacob Gross had evangelized in Lahr before arriving in Strasbourg. Sattler went there after his stay in Strasbourg. Here, he did some evangelism and won at least one convert to Anabaptism. He seems to have had a conflict with the local Protestant pastor, Jakob Ottelinus, who complained about Sattler (and the Anabaptists in general) in a letter to Martin Bucer:

> In Christ's name I consider these men [the Anabaptists] to be most pernicious for the edification particularly of those who are feeble of conscience, since the Anabaptists compel those who are now contrite in heart and humiliated by God to satisfy the law to the last measure. . . . The grace of Christ promised to Paul in the days of old is not sufficient for them, but rather these hangmen try to restrain the impulse by the weight of the law enforced by Moses. O most evil pharisaism! Foremost in this matter is Michael, formerly a monk at St. Peter's, the most stubborn of all, who concedes to no one, condemns all magistracy, obliges no one, even if (because of the demands of charity) he flatters on occasion; he is in fact terrible, horrible and of impetuous voice when arraigned for his insolence; moreover, in consequence

---

6   *Ibid.*

of his monastic position he attacks the one bringing him scriptures and reproaches him for being an adherent of the dead letter, and instead of the adduced argument, he claims that the spirit has revealed to him all things needful; by his own spirit he distorts all things because his opinion is founded on itself. . . .There is a certain man in the neighborhood near me, a pious man—had he not been seduced by these impostors—a man whom I had earlier educated in the gospel as a small favor, as if he were a catecumen [*sic*] in the matter of faith. Led I know not by what spirit, he gave himself wholly to the Anabaptists, and turned away from me completely as a person skilled in the impiety of this world, who was enmeshed in the affairs of this world. Moreover, it came to pass a few days ago that when his wife had given birth to a child, he refused, at the instigation of Michael, to purify the child with the baptism of water—for which reason our officers and council, after deliberation about the situation and examination of the case, ruled that he have his child baptized according to custom.[7]

This negative evaluation of Michael's character, polemical as it was, is hardly to be taken as absolutely true; however, some interesting information is provided. For instance, we learn that Michael was steadfast under the attempts of Protestant theologians to convince him that obedience to God is not necessary for salvation. Notice also that Ottelinus classes Michael's insistence on obedience to Christ and the Apostles as restraining by "the weight of the law enforced by Moses"—while it was Moses' Law that the Protestants were following (on such subjects as war and the oath) while the Anabaptists submitted to the higher law of Christ.

It is doubtful whether Michael actually claimed that "the spirit has revealed to him all things needful" by some sort of

---

7   C. Arnold Snyder, *The Life and Thought of Michael Sattler*, © 1984, Herald Press (Scottdale, PA 15683), p. 95. Used by permission.

direct, special revelation. There is no other evidence that he did so, and his constant appeal to Scripture in all other sources by or about him make it clear that God's written Word was his final authority, not any extra-Biblical "revelation." Nevertheless, the Anabaptists are known to have put emphasis upon the guidance and activity of the Holy Spirit; thus, to find Sattler emphasizing the confirmation of the Spirit for his teachings does not seem out-of-place.

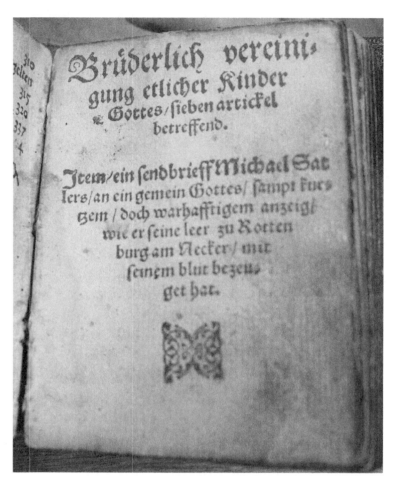

Title page of a printed copy of the
Schleitheim Confession from the mid-1500s.

5
Schleitheim

he disunity and confusion among Anabaptists could not have escaped Michael Sattler's attention. He had evangelized in the canton of Zürich, where persecution was causing some Anabaptists to go off the deep end. In Strasbourg, he had met Ludwig Haetzer, a friend of Hans Denck, who was marginally involved with the Anabaptist movement but was a spiritualist and morally impure. He may have met Hans Denck, with his spiritualizing tendencies; even if not, he surely knew of Denck and his teachings. The lack of conviction for nonresistance on the part of some Anabaptists, such as the followers of Hubmaier, surely troubled Sattler deeply.

He was not alone. The subjects covered in the Schleitheim Confession and Sattler's letter to the Strasbourg reformers seem to have been extensively discussed by him with other Anabaptists; Sattler's letter to the reformers says that the convictions reflected therein were ones "which I together with my brothers and sisters have understood out of

Scripture."[1] Perhaps a consensus was growing among those Anabaptists in contact with Sattler in the months leading up to the Schleitheim Conference. Perhaps Michael had already drafted the Schleitheim Confession prior to the conference.

In any case, Michael's concerns for scriptural unity and vision must have been shared by many others, and someone had the idea of calling a conference of Anabaptists to gather and come to agreement. Schleitheim on the Border, north of Zürich and not far from the former Anabaptist strongholds of Waldshut and Schaffhausen, was chosen as the location for the meeting. Following the decision to call the meeting, messengers would have to go out to the scattered churches in Switzerland and southern Germany, calling the believers to Schleitheim and probably giving them some idea of what was to be discussed.

No one knew if this was going to work. The minds of Michael Sattler and his fellow-organizers must have been filled with questions. Would the messengers find receptive hearers, and would the Anabaptists actually make the risky trip to Schleitheim? Would government agents arrest the messengers, torture them, and extract information about the planned meeting, endangering everyone? Would this meeting actually be possible? Would it be disrupted while in progress and everyone arrested?

No one knew if this was going to work. Even if there were no disruptions to their plans, would the attendants at the meeting be able to come to agreement? Or might the meeting push them deeper into division, entrenching people in their various opinions? If the delegates were able to come to agreement, would they be able to bring their congregations along when they went home, and the whole church come to unity?

---

1   John Howard Yoder, translator and editor, *The Legacy of Michael Sattler,* © 1973, Herald Press (Scottdale, PA 15683), pp. 21-22. Used by permission.

The inside of the Täuferhöhle (Anabaptist cave), where Anabaptists met in secret for worship.

Despite the many questions, Michael and his friends did not allow fear to paralyze them. In great faith, they called the meeting.

The Schleitheim Confession

In February, 1527, Swiss and south German Anabaptists secretly gathered in a brother's home in Schleitheim. Apparently the messengers were able to spread the news without being caught, and the meeting happened without the knowledge of the persecuting authorities. Outward peace from their enemies foreshadowed the peace which would prevail within.

Sadly, almost nothing is known about the events of the Schleitheim Conference, nor do we know who attended it. We do know that the delegates came to agreement and unity, and that their shared convictions on baptism, the ban, the Lord's Supper, separation from the world, shepherds in the church, the sword, and the oath were written down as the Schleitheim Confession—which they titled *Brotherly Union of a Number of Children of God Concerning Seven Articles.* Michael Sattler probably wrote the confession itself, but it reflects the conclusions of the group. Michael also wrote a cover letter for the confession, explaining the meeting and its purpose for those who had not attended.

Michael's cover letter acknowledged that "It is also apparent with what cunning the devil has turned us aside, so that he might destroy and bring to an end the work of God which in mercy and grace has been partly begun in us." Despite this, Michael was confident that "Christ, the true Shepherd of our souls, Who has begun this in us, will certainly direct the same and teach [us] to His honor and our salvation, Amen."[2]

The devil's cunning was manifest in that "A very great offense has been introduced by certain false brethren among us, so that some have turned aside from the faith, in the way they intend to practice and observe the freedom of the Spirit and of Christ." This freedom, however, was not the freedom of Christ: "But such have missed the truth and to their condemnation are given over to the lasciviousness and self-indulgence of the flesh. They think faith and love may do and permit everything, and nothing will harm them nor condemn them, since they are believers."

These words sound very similar to the teachings of Martin Bucer and Wolfgang Capito, who had just a few weeks before been insisting to Michael that "faith and love" permitted one to ignore the plain commandments of Scripture. Although Michael may have had them in mind, it seems

---

2   All Schleitheim quotes in this book from John C. Wenger, "The Schleitheim Confession of Faith," *Mennonite Quarterly Review* 19(4) (October 1945):243-253.

that the "false brethren" were Anabaptists, since they were described as "among us." In the postscript to the Confession, Michael says the "brethren who had heretofore been in error" had caused many "weaker consciences" to be perplexed and "the Name of God to be greatly slandered." Thus, "Therefore there has been a great need for us to become of one mind in the Lord, which has come to pass."

These "false brethren," then, seem to be some among the Anabaptists who accepted reasoning like that of Capito and Bucer. Fanatics like those in Grüningen, who acted in bizarre ways, and those such as Balthasar Hubmaier, who accepted the sword, may also have been in Sattler's mind as he wrote. Michael pointed out that faith and love did not produce sinful living.

> Observe, you who are God's members in Christ Jesus, that faith in the Heavenly Father through Jesus Christ does not take such form. It does not produce and result in such things as these false brethren and sisters do and teach. Guard yourselves and be warned of such people, for they do not serve our Father, but their father, the devil.

> But you are not that way. For they that are Christ's have crucified the flesh with its passions and lusts. You understand me well and [know] the brethren whom we mean. Separate yourselves from them for they are perverted. Petition the Lord that they may have the knowledge which leads to repentance, and [pray] for us that we may have constancy to persevere in the way which we have espoused, for the honor of God and of Christ, His Son, Amen.

In seven articles, the assembled group then described its agreement and unity. The first three articles describe the composition of the church; last three, the actions and ethics of the church.

Aerial view of the village of Schleitheim.

The first article, on baptism, states that baptism would be given only to those who had "learned repentance and amendment of life" and who "walk in the resurrection of Jesus Christ, and wish to be buried with Him in death, so that they may be resurrected with Him." This made entrance into the church via baptism available only to those who had been truly born again, rather than, as in the case of infant baptism, to everyone—whether they would eventually follow Jesus or not.

Article 2 is on the ban, or excommunication. An examination was to be made before the Lord's Supper, "so that we may break and eat one bread, with one mind and in one love, and may drink of one cup." Those who "are baptized into the one body of Christ . . . yet who slip sometimes and fall into error and sin" should be admonished and, if unrepentant, should be excommunicated. This allows the congregation to share the Lord's Supper in unity.

The Lord's Supper is discussed next, in Article 3. Only baptized members of the "one body of Christ which is the church of God" are allowed to partake of communion. Article 1 had defined those who were allowed to be baptized as those who had repented and learned amendment of life, buried and spiritually resurrected with Jesus to new and spiritual life. These were the people allowed to take communion with the church, because one cannot sit at the table of the Lord and that of devils. "Therefore all who follow the devil and the world have no part with those who are called unto God out of the world." Those who have "been called by one God to one faith, to one baptism, to one Spirit, to one body, with all the children of God's church" can be "made [into] one bread with them," in the joyful celebration of the church's unity in Christ which is the Lord's Supper.

These first three articles have explained who the members of the true church are. Articles 5-7 explain the ethics and actions of this church.

Article 5, on shepherds or pastors in the church, says that the shepherd should be one who has a good report of those outside the church and who can "in all things . . . see to the care of the body of Christ, in order that it may be built up and developed," including preaching, admonition, disciplining, leading in prayer, and presiding at communion. The congregation which chose him should provide for the pastor's needs. The congregation, however, has the right to discipline him if necessary, on the testimony of two or three witnesses. If the pastor is martyred, another should be immediately appointed "so that God's little flock and people may not be destroyed."

Article 6, on the sword, and Article 7, on the oath, are on subjects which had been controversial among Anabaptists before the Schleitheim meeting. The Anabaptists gathered at Schleitheim came to a strong conviction for nonresistance and nonparticipation in earthly governments, saying that "The sword is ordained of God outside the perfection of Christ." The "perfection of Christ" is the church, in which "only the ban is used for a warning and for the excommunication of the one who has sinned, without putting the flesh to death,—simply the warning and the command to sin no more." The worldly magistrate, however, has the sword "for the punishment of the wicked and for their death." Since Christ "teaches and commands us to learn of Him, for He is meek and lowly in heart," the true Christian must follow His example of love and mercy, not taking up the sword of government to punish wrongdoing. Jury duty and all service as magistrates was forbidden.

Article 7 forbade oaths, which was extremely counter-cultural. Medieval society ran on oaths. To refuse to take oaths would instantly mark one out as a "heretic"—and arrest, torture, and execution could follow. Yet the Schleitheim Anabaptists recognized that "Christ, who teaches the perfection of the Law, prohibits all swearing to His [followers], whether true or false."

Article 4, on separation from the world, comes in the center of the Schleitheim Confession, and it philosophically and theologically undergirds the entire structure. The rest does not make sense without the foundational concepts of Article 4.

Central to Article 4 is the conviction that there are only two types of people in the world—believers and unbelievers.

> A separation shall be made from the evil and from the wickedness which the devil planted in the world; in this manner, simply that we shall not have fellowship with them [the wicked] and not run with them in the multitude of their abominations. This is the way it is: Since all who do not walk in the obedience of faith, and have not united themselves with God so that they wish to do His will, are a great abomination before God, it is not possible for anything to grow or issue from them

except abominable things. For truly all creatures are in but two classes, good and bad, believing and unbelieving, darkness and light, the world and those who [have come] out of the world, God's temple and idols, Christ and Belial; and none can have part with the other.

Because of this, "To us then the command of the Lord is clear when He calls upon us to be separate from the evil and thus He will be our God and we shall be His sons and daughters." Thus, the creation of a church like that described in the first three articles makes sense—composed of people who have been born again, have repented and changed their lives, who mutually admonish each other to avoid sin, and who live in peace, love, and unity (as symbolized in the Lord's Supper). Article 4 goes on to say:

From all this we should learn that everything which is not united with our God and Christ cannot be other than an abomination which we should shun and flee from. By this is meant all popish and antipopish works and church services, meetings and church attendance, drinking houses, civic affairs, the commitments [made in] unbelief and other things of that kind, which are highly regarded by the world and yet are carried on in flat contradiction to the command of God, in accordance with all the unrighteousness which is in the world.

The separate church lives in a distinctive, nonconformed way. This avoidance of "everything which is not united with our God" supports the practices of the next three articles, particularly nonresistance and non-swearing of oaths. In fact, Article 4 closes with the first mention of nonresistance in the Confession, thus showing that war and violence were seen as chief marks of the world from which the Christian must be separate.

Therefore there will also unquestionably fall from us the unchristian, devilish weapons of force—such as sword, armor and the like, and all their use [either] for friends or against one's enemies—by virtue of the word of Christ, Resist not [him that is] evil.

"Therefore there will also unquestionably fall from us the unchristian, devilish weapons of force—such as sword, armor and the like."

Defining the Church

In sweeping and compelling terms, the Schleitheim Confession defined the true church. It was not to be, as Hubmaier and his followers thought, a state church, supported by the coercion and force of the government. It was not to live carelessly using "faith and love" as an excuse for sinful living. It was not to focus, as Hut did, on end-times prophecies and setting dates for Jesus' return and the violent revenge of the saints.

This view of the church also contrasted with what Sattler would have embraced as a monk. Monasticism viewed itself as "the perfect" who lived out Jesus' "counsels of perfection" in the midst of an imperfect and less-ethically rigorous church. The dualism or contrast was between *ecclesia* and *ecclesiola*—the large, main church and the little, purer church within it, although both in fellowship with each other. In Schleitheim, *all* Christians must live up to the teachings and follow the example of Jesus, not just the special, spiritual "elite." The dualism or contrast was now between the church and the world. There is no room in the Schleitheim world-view for middle ground. Those who do not obey and follow Jesus are not true Christians.

Completely at Peace

The conference had actually happened. No one had known whether the authorities would prevent the meeting and martyr the delegates; whether delegates would come; or whether the delegates would be able to reach agreement. Once they had reached agreement, the Schleitheim Confession was written and endorsed by the gathering. Michael wrote a cover letter and postscript to be circulated with it, stating the reasons for the gathering and Confession and urging other Anabaptists to accept the decisions and unity of the Schleitheim gathering. (The full text of the confession and Michael's cover letter and postscript begin on page 113.) What could easily have degenerated into argument and further division had resulted in peace, agreement, and unity. "In this," Michael wrote, "we have perceived the oneness of the

From Schleitheim to Menno

The brother who owned the house in Schleitheim at which the meeting occurred lived long enough to, in 1557, attend a Swiss Brethren ministers' meeting at which the delegates wrote a letter to Menno Simons. The letter states, "And a teacher was with us from Michael Sattler's time, and the agreement of Michael Sattler was drawn up in his house; he has been in the faith more than thirty years."[1] This letter confirms Michael Sattler's association with Schleitheim.

---

1   Zylis Jacobs and Lemke Cramer, Letter to Menno Simons; translation from C. Arnold Snyder, editor, *Later Writings of the Swiss Anabaptists 1529-1592*, 2017, Pandora Press, p. 90.

Spirit of our Father and of our common Christ with us." The conference had ended "completely at peace," and agreement had been made "without the contradiction of any brethren."

"The hangman will prove it to you,
he can debate with you, arch heretic!"

"I appeal to Scripture."

6
The Burning Testimony

$\mathcal{I}$n the form of the Schleitheim Confession, the Anabaptists now had the compelling, Scriptural vision they badly needed. Only a few short months after the Schleitheim Conference, Michael Sattler dramatically personified that vision in a nonresistant martyrdom, giving a powerful testimony to his convictions.

After the Schleitheim Conference, Michael Sattler made his way—probably in the company of Wilhelm Reublin—to the town of Horb on the Neckar River, where an Anabaptist congregation already existed. He seems to have been chosen to serve as the congregation's "shepherd," either once he arrived there or at Schleitheim. His time of service in this role was to prove a very short one. Within days of arriving, Anabaptist hunters arrested more than a dozen Anabaptists in the town, including Michael and Margaretha Sattler. Several of the prisoners, including the Sattlers, were taken by armed knights to the town of Binsdorf, about ten miles from Horb, where they were imprisoned in a tower.

The town of Horb am Neckar, where Michael Sattler served as "shepherd" of an Anabaptist congregation for a few days.

The town of Horb was under the political rule of Count Joachim of Zollern, a representative of Archduke Ferdinand of Austria. The archduke was a militant Catholic determined to keep his lands free of "heresy." Soon after the arrest, he was informed of the prisoners who had been taken, and preparations for a trial began.

Holding a trial was easier said than done. The trial date was originally set for April 12, 1527, but various obstacles were encountered and the date had to be postponed to May 17. They planned to hold the trial in the Austrian town of Rottenburg on the Neckar; eight Anabaptists had already been arrested there prior to the Schleitheim conference. The authorities were trying to negotiate with the University of Tübingen, asking them to send two representatives to participate in the trial. The university refused, because, as Roman Catholic clergy, they were not allowed to take part in trials which resulted in a death sentence. Finally, on May 6, they sent two doctors of the arts to serve as their representatives.

Ferdinand

Michael Sattler was arrested in Austria, which was under the rule of Archduke Ferdinand. Ferdinand was a member of the Habsburg family, which since 1437 had held the throne of the Holy Roman Empire and had been gaining increasing political power and influence in Europe. Through a strategic marriage, Ferdinand added Austria and Bohemia to the Habsburg holdings, taking the crown as king of Hungary in 1526. His brother, Charles V, was king of Spain and was elected Holy Roman Emperor in 1519. Busy with his Spanish kingdom, Charles left much of

Ferdinand I in 1531.

the work of governing the German nation to Ferdinand. In 1558, Charles abdicated the crown and Ferdinand was elected Holy Roman Emperor.

Both brothers were devoted Catholics and hated "heresy" in all its forms. They persecuted Protestants, Anabaptists, and all other dissenters. The persecution against Anabaptists in Ferdinand's lands resulted in the martyrdoms of Michael Sattler, George Blaurock, Jakob Hutter, and hundreds more.

Questioned Under Torture

While generally viewed with repugnance today, questioning prisoners under torture was common in the sixteenth century. Supposedly, the torture would motivate the accused to tell the truth, or (in the case of religious prisoners such as Anabaptists) encourage them to recant their faith or give information about other "heretics."

The most often-mentioned types of torture used on Anabaptist prisoners were whipping and the rack.

The rack was a device built on a ladder or a table, on which the prisoner was laid. His ankles and wrists were tied with ropes to two rollers on opposite ends of the machine. These rollers then retracted the ropes, stretching the prisoner's

The rack.

limbs and putting extreme stress on the joints, sometimes dislocating them. Some prisoners fainted; some recanted or gave information; others stood firm through the torture.

A variation on the theme was tying a prisoner by one hand to the ceiling rafters and hanging weights from his feet.

We do not know how Michael Sattler was tortured; some or all of these methods may have been used. Nevertheless, he stayed true to his faith no matter what his persecutors did to him.

In the meantime, some of the prisoners, including Michael, were questioned under torture and threatened with death. Michael was questioned about his views on baptism, the Lord's Supper, extreme unction, the saints, the Turks, swearing of oaths, and why he had left the monastery. He told his questioners that a saint is one "who keeps God's commands here on earth and who, for God's sake, patiently suffers adversity, anxiety and tribulation." He said he had left the monastery because "he had seen that the pope and bishops, monks and nuns were greedy, proud, envious, immoral and fornicators and full of evil; therefore he had not wished to be in the cloister any longer, and had married and hoped to be saved in this state."[1] (The text of the pre-trial questioning is on page 135).

While imprisoned at Binsdorf, Michael Sattler—knowing his death was near—wrote a farewell letter to his congregation at Horb (the full text begins on page 125). He encouraged them to remain faithful to Christ at any cost, and not to give up the fight for eternal life because of suffering. He also warned against false brethren who "have fallen short of this love," becoming "puffed up . . . and useless with vain speculation and understanding of those things which God wants to keep secret to Himself."[2] This sounds like the secret doctrines of the end times which Hans Hut taught to special initiates. Hut and others like him may have been the false brothers who Sattler had in mind. Michael continues:

> I do not admonish or reject the grace and revelation of God, but the inflated use of this revelation. What is the use, says Paul, if one speaks with all sorts of tongues of men and angels? And knows all mysteries, wisdom, and has all faith, he says, what is all that worth if the one and

---

1   C. Arnold Snyder, "Rottenburg Revisited: New Evidence Concerning the Trial of Michael Sattler," *Mennonite Quarterly Review* 54(3) (July 1980):208-228, p. 213. (Hereafter referenced as Snyder, "Rottenburg.")
2   John Howard Yoder, translator and editor, *The Legacy of Michael Sattler*, © 1973, Herald Press (Scottdale, PA 15683), pp. 59-60. Used by permission.

only love is not exercised? You have experienced what such puffed up speech and unwisdom have brought to birth. You still see daily their false fruits, whether they have abandoned themselves completely to God.

Let no one shift your goal, which has been set in the letter of the Holy Scripture, which is sealed by the blood of Christ and of many witnesses of Jesus. Do not listen what they say from their father, for he is a deceiver, believe not their spirit, for it is completely submerged in the flesh. Judge what I write you, take the matter to heart, so that this abomination may be separated from you and you might be found to be the humble, fruitful, and obedient children of God.[3]

Michael then informed his readers about the circumstances of the prisoners and encouraged his congregation to stay faithful to the Lord.

You have probably learned from brothers how some of ours have been taken prisoner and then, when the brothers had also been taken prisoner in Horb, how we were taken to Binsdorf. During this time we underwent all sorts of attacks from the adversaries. They menaced us once with a cord, then with fire, then with the sword. In such dangers I completely abandoned myself to the Lord in His will and readied myself for death for the sake of His testimony, with all my brothers and my wife. Then I thought of the great number of false brothers and of you who are so few, yea, such a small band; and how few faithful workers there are in the vineyard of the Lord. So it seemed needful to me to urge you by this exhortation to follow us in God's combat and thereby to console you that you might not become weary under the discipline of the Lord.

---

3   *Ibid.*, p. 60.

In sum: dear brothers and sisters, this letter shall be my farewell from all of you who truly love and follow God (I do not know the others), and a testimony of my love toward you, which God has put in my heart for the sake of your salvation. I would have desired, and, I might hope, it would have been useful, that I had been able to continue for a little time longer to work at the Lord's task, but it is better for my sake to be released and with Christ to await the hope of the blessed. The Lord can certainly raise up for Himself another laborer to complete His work. Pray that reapers may be driven out into the harvest, for the time of threshing has come near. The abomination of desolation is visible among you. The elect servants and maidservants of God will be marked on the forehead with the name of their Father. The world has arisen against those who are redeemed from its error. The gospel is testified to before all the world for a testimony. According to this the day of the Lord must no longer tarry.[4]

On Trial

On May 15, the court began to assemble for the trial. On the same day, Archduke Ferdinand wrote a letter to the officials in Hohenberg, recommending that Michael Sattler receive the punishment of a "third baptism" (drowning)—without a trial.

His advice arrived too late to be acted upon, and a trial was held. Twenty-four judges heard the trial and decided the case. The trial was held in Rottenburg on May 17 and 18, 1527. About twenty prisoners were on trial, including Michael Sattler, his wife, two other Anabaptists from Horb, and several from Rottenburg. Sattler and his three companions had been brought from Binsdorf, escorted by 24 horsemen.

---

4   *Ibid.*, pp. 60-61.

Count Joachim ordered 56 extra foot soldiers to be present in Rottenburg during the trial, in case the locals rebelled at the execution.

The trial opened Friday, May 17. The court requested the prisoners to choose an advocate for themselves. Michael Sattler replied, "You servants of God! I am not willing to contend legally with anyone, therefore I need no advocate."[5] He later added that when the legal accusations concerned God's Word, they were forbidden to dispute; however, they wished to be persuaded by the Scriptures if they were in error.

Then the city clerk of Ensisheim, Eberhard Hoffman, read the official charges against the prisoners. The charges said that the accused "have dared to establish a new sect and unchristian rite contrary to the holy Christian faith, contrary to all order and law of the holy Christian Church, by their own decision and against the published Imperial and Royal mandate and command."[6] The charges said that the accused did not believe in the Catholic doctrine of the Lord's Supper, in infant baptism, extreme unction, and that they despised Mary and the saints. (The full text of the official charges is on page 139).

After the official charges were read, there were many delays, and Michael probably did not get to give his defense until the second day of the trial. At that time, Michael requested that the charges be read again. The account of the trial as given by Klaus von Graveneck, one of the soldiers, reads:

> When I first came, Michael Sattler requested, since the matter had now moved on for several hours, the articles being many, that [the articles] be read to him again so that he might be heard further thereon;[7] against which

---

5   Snyder, "Rottenburg," p. 216.

6   *Ibid.*, p. 214.

7   Foregoing from Snyder, "Rottenburg," p. 226.

the *Schultheiss* (as the advocate of his lord) objected and did not wish to grant. Michael thereupon asked for a ruling. When the judges had taken counsel, the answer was that, insofar as the prosecution would be willing to permit this, the judges would find it proper. Thereupon the *Stadtschreiber* of Ensisheim [Eberhard Hoffman], as speaker of the said advocate, spoke as follows: "Provident, honorable, and wise lords, he has boasted that he has the Holy Spirit, therefore it would seem to me not to be necessary to grant him this; for if he has the Holy Spirit, as he boasts, the Spirit should be able to tell him what is in the indictment."

To this Michael Sattler answered: "Ye servants of God, I hope that this will not be denied to me; for the stated points of accusation do not all concern me and I do not know what they are."

Answer of the *Stadtschreiber*: "Provident, honorable, and wise lords, although we are not obligated to do so, we are willing out of generosity to concede this to him, so that, in his heresy, it may not be thought that he has been subjected to injustice or that anyone desires to be unfair to him, therefore let the articles be read again to him orally."[8]

The charges were then given, but it was a summary of the charges rather than the full, official charges. von Graveneck records the charges read at this point as follows:

1. That he and his associates have acted against imperial mandate.

2. He has taught, held, and believed, that the body and blood of Christ are not in the sacrament.

---

8   John Howard Yoder, translator and editor, *The Legacy of Michael Sattler*, © 1973, Herald Press (Scottdale, PA 15683), p. 70. Used by permission.

3. He taught and believes that infant baptism is not requisite toward salvation.

4. They have rejected the sacrament of unction.

5. Despised and scorned the mother of God and the saints.

6. They have said that one should not swear to the government.

7. Initiated a new and unheard-of usage in the Lord's Supper, with wine and bread crumbled in a basin, and eating the same.

8. He has forsaken the order and has married a wife.

9. He has said: "If the Turk were to come into the land, one should not resist him, and, if it were right to wage war, he would rather go to war against the Christians than against the Turks," which is after all a great offense, to take the side of the greatest enemy of our holy faith against us.[9]

A charge about the oath (#6) has now been added which was not present in the official charges, but was brought up at Sattler's pretrial hearing. The seventh charge, and the final two charges against Sattler personally, have also been added.

Having heard the charges again, Michael Sattler asked to consult with his brothers and sisters, which was granted. After a short consultation with them, Michael fearlessly took the floor and began his defense.

You servants of God!

Since now for the third time the court has refused to hear my answer and that of my brothers and sisters, and

---

9   John Howard Yoder, translator and editor, *The Legacy of Michael Sattler,* © 1973, Herald Press (Scottdale, PA 15683), pp. 70-71. Used by permission.

that answer is detained until the present, we say that this charge touches upon the only, eternal Word of God and God has forbidden his Word to be tried according to the flesh; therefore they do not wish to dispute but rather wish to testify with the eternal and true Word of God.[10]

Concerning the articles which have to do with me, my brothers and sisters, hear the following brief statement:

1. We do not admit that we have acted counter to the imperial mandate; for it says that one should not adhere to the Lutheran doctrine and seduction, but only to the gospel and the Word of God; this we have held to. Counter to the gospel and the Word of God I do not know that I have done anything; in witness thereto I appeal to the words of Christ.

Extreme Unction

The fourth charge against Michael Sattler and his fellow-prisoners was that they had rejected "the sacrament of unction." In his response, Michael said they had not rejected oil, but the pope's attempt to "improve" it, and that James's words about anointing do not refer to the pope's sacrament.

The Catholic sacrament referred to was once known as "Extreme Unction," now known as "Last Rites" or "Last Sacraments." Given to those who are elderly, sick, or near death, a priest will administer the Last Rites which consist of three elements: 1) Penance; 2) Anointing with Oil; and 3) Communion. Catholics believe this is a final infusion of grace before the dying man leaves this world, preparing him for the trip to eternity with his sins forgiven and (hopefully) a short time in the fires of Purgatory.

---

10   Foregoing from Snyder, "Rottenburg," p. 217.

The Turk

"The Turk," said the court official summarizing the charges against Michael Sattler, is "the greatest enemy of our holy faith."

For centuries, Roman Catholic Europe had been at war with Islamic armies in the Middle East, Africa, Spain, and eastern Europe. In Michael Sattler's day, "the Turks"—Muslims from Turkey, the Ottoman Empire—were threatening the eastern border of the Habsburg Empire, the dynasty of Archduke Ferdinand and his brother, the Emperor Charles V, which had arrested Michael and put him on trial. The Ottoman Turks were indeed a great threat to the Habsburgs which they took very seriously.

Fighting under their ruler, Suleiman the Magnificent (pictured), who fancied himself an Islamic Alexander the Great, the Ottomans attempted to set up a single Islamic Ottoman Empire from India to Germany. They advanced across eastern Europe, absorbing several European nations. At the Battle of Mohács in 1526 (just the year before Sattler's trial), Suleiman—with an army of nearly half a million—completely defeated the 25,000 man Hungarian army, including killing the king of Hungary. About 23,000 Hungarians were killed in the battle itself, with the remaining 2,000 taken prisoner and, the next day, paraded before Suleiman and beheaded, after which the Turks looted and burned the Hungarian towns of Buda and Pest. For Michael to call the Catholics "spiritual Turks" was a very graphic image indeed, to say the least.

The crown of Hungary went to Archduke Ferdinand, the Hungarian king's brother-in-law. The Turks continued to advance, and in 1529, Suleiman was at the walls of Vienna, Austria, Ferdinand's capital.

It "is after all a great offense, to take the side of the greatest enemy of our holy faith against us," they had said at Sattler's trial. Apparently the pretender to the Hungarian throne, who had battled with Ferdinand between the Turkish onslaughts, did not understand this. His army was encamped outside the walls of Vienna with Suleiman's.

King Ferdinand was able to repulse the Turkish attack, but Suleiman promised to return, doing so in 1532. He was again repulsed, with the aid of Emperor Charles V, Ferdinand's brother. In 1562, after continued fighting, Ferdinand paid Suleiman an annual tribute to keep the peace. The Turks were not finally pushed back until 1683.

The Hungarian pretender was not the only Catholic to join forces with the Turks. In 1544, Francis I, king of France, and Pope Paul III allied with Suleiman against Emperor Charles V. Surrounded on all sides—the French to the west, the Turks to the east, and the pope further south—Charles needed all the soldiers he could get. He needed the German princes to provide the troops, money, and materials needed to fight on all sides. In order to do this, he temporarily made peace with the Protestant nobles, and German Catholic and German Protestant alike fought against Catholic French and Italians and Muslim Turks. The pope himself had taken the side of the Turks, doing what the Austrian court found so offensive when Michael Sattler had merely suggested such a thing.

Charles won the war. With peace on all sides, he then turned to the Protestants within, and—now with the support of the pope!—fought an inner-German war against the Protestant princes, winning it as well. However, he was never able to stamp out Protestantism completely, nor was his brother and successor as emperor, Ferdinand.

2. That the real body of Christ the Lord is not in the sacrament, we admit: for Scripture says: Christ has ascended to heaven and sits at the right hand of His heavenly Father, whence He shall come to judge the living and the dead. It follows therefrom, since He is in heaven and not in the bread, that He cannot be eaten bodily.

3. Regarding baptism we say: infant baptism is not useful toward salvation, for it stands written, that we live only by faith. Further: "He who believes and is baptized, will be saved." Peter says in 1 Peter 3: "which also now saves you in baptism, which thereby signifies not the laying off of filth of the flesh but the covenant of a good conscience with God through the resurrection of Christ."

4. We have not rejected oil, for it is a creature of God. What God has made is good and not to be rejected. But what pope, bishop, monks, and priests have wanted to do to improve on it, this we think nothing of. For the pope has never made anything good. What the epistle of James speaks of is not the pope's oil.

5. We have not dishonored the mother of God and the saints; rather the mother of Christ is to be praised above all women because to her was given the grace that she could give birth to the Savior of the whole world. That she, however, is a mediatrix and advocate, the Scripture knows nothing of; for she must like us await judgment. Paul says to Timothy that Christ is our mediator and advocate before God. Concerning the saints, we say that we who live and believe are the saints. I testify to this with the epistle of Paul to the Romans, Corinthians, Ephesians, and elsewhere: he always writes: "To the beloved saints." Therefore we, who believe, are the saints. Those who have died in the faith we call the "blessed."

6. We hold that one should not swear allegiance to government for the Lord says in Matthew 5: "You should swear no oath, but your speech shall be yea, yea, nay, nay."

7. When God called me to testify to His Word, and I read Paul, I considered the unchristian and dangerous estate in which I had been, in view of the pomp, pride, usury, and great fornication of the monks and priests. I therefore obeyed and took a wife according to the command of God. Paul was prophesying well on the subject to Timothy: "In the last days it shall come to pass that they will forbid marriage and food, which God has created that they might be enjoyed with thanksgiving."

8. If the Turk comes, he should not be resisted, for it stands written: thou shalt not kill. We should not defend ourselves against the Turks or our other persecutors, but with fervent prayer should implore God that He might be our defense and our resistance. As to me saying that if waging war were proper I would rather take the field against the so-called Christians who persecute, take captive, and kill true Christians, than against the Turks, this was for the following reason: the Turk is a genuine Turk and knows nothing of the Christian faith. He is a Turk according to the flesh. But you claim to be Christians, boast of Christ, and still persecute the faithful witnesses of Christ. Thus you are Turks according to the Spirit.

To conclude: you servants of God, I admonish you to consider whereto you have been established by God to punish evil, to defend and protect the just. Since, then, we have done nothing counter to God and the gospel, consider therefore what you are doing. You should also ask, and you will find, that I and my brothers and sisters have not acted against any government in words or deeds.

Therefore, you servants of God, in case you might not have heard or read the Word of God, would you send for the most learned [men] and for the godly books of the Bible, in whatever language they might be, and let them discuss the same with us in the Word of God. If they show us with Holy Scripture that we are in error and wrong, we will gladly retract and recant, and will gladly suffer condemnation and the punishment for our offense. But if we cannot be proved in error, I hope to God that you will repent and let yourselves be taught.[11]

On hearing this, the judges laughed and Eberhard Hoffman said, "O yes, you disreputable, desperate, and mischievous monk, you think we should debate with you? Sure enough, the hangman will debate with you, you can believe me."[12] Sattler replied, "What God wills, that will come to pass."[13]

Clerk: "It would have been good if you had never been born."

Michael: "God knows what is good."

Clerk: "You arch-heretic, you have seduced pious people; if they would only give up their errors and ask for grace."

Michael: "Grace is in God alone."

Another one of the prisoners said, "One should not deviate from the truth."

Prosecutor: "You desperate evil doer and arch heretic, I tell you this: if there were no hangmen here I would hang you myself and would be sure I would be serving God thereby."

Michael: "God will judge rightly."

Hoffman finally seemed to grow tired of this debate—or possibly he saw that his bad manners were making an un-

---

11   John Howard Yoder, translator and editor, *The Legacy of Michael Sattler*, © 1973, Herald Press (Scottdale, PA 15683), pp. 71-73. Used by permission.

12   *Ibid.*, p. 73.

13   *Ibid.*

favorable impression—so he exchanged a few words with Sattler in Latin. Finally, he said to the judges, "This kind of talk could go on all day: therefore, Lord Judge, would you proceed with the verdict, I rest the case."[14] The judges then asked Michael Sattler if he also rested the case, to which he replied:

> You servants of God, I have not been sent to defend the Word of God in court. We are sent to testify thereto. Therefore we cannot consent to any legal process, for we have no such command from God. If, however, we have not been able to be justly convinced, we are ready to suffer, for the Word of God, whatever will and may be laid upon us to suffer, all for our faith in Christ Jesus our Savior, as long as we have in us a breath of life, unless we should be convinced otherwise with Scripture.[15]

The city clerk said, "The hangman will prove it to you, he can debate with you, arch heretic." Sattler replied, "I appeal to Scripture."[16]

At this, the judges rose and went to another room. There they deliberated for one and a half hours. During this time, Michael had to endure much from his enemies in the courtroom. One said, "If I see that you get out of this, I'll believe in you. How could you mislead yourself and these others and seduce them in this way?" He then took a sword which was lying on the table, partly unsheathed it, and said, "See, with this we will debate with you." Michael was silent; one of the other Anabaptists said, "Do not throw pearls before swine." Then one of the men in the court asked Michael why he had not stayed as a lord in the monastery, to which he replied, "According to the flesh I would be a lord but it is better as it is."[17]

---

14   *Ibid.*, p. 73-74.
15   *Ibid.*, p. 74.
16   *Ibid.*
17   *Ibid.*

The judges finally emerged from their deliberation and passed the following sentence:

> In the matter of the prosecutor of the imperial majesty versus Michael Sattler, it has been found that Michael Sattler should be given into the hands of the hangman, who shall lead him to the square and cut off his tongue, then chain him to a wagon, there tear his body twice with red hot tongs, and again when he is brought before the gate, five more times. When this is done to be burned to powder as a heretic.[18]

Execution

Following the sentencing, Michael joyfully comforted his wife before the judges and rulers. He was then taken to a room where he was able to talk with the prosecutor, whom he admonished to repent:

> Schultheiss [advocate/prosecutor], you know that you and your fellow judges have condemned me contrary to justice and without proof, therefore look out, and repent, for if not, you and they will be eternally condemned before the judgment of God to eternal fire.[19]

Sattler was then taken back to prison, where he waited until Monday, May 20, 1527. What struggles he may have faced through those two nights and a day, waiting for the gruesome sentence to be carried out, we do not know. When he was led into the marketplace for his execution on Monday morning, he was as fearless as he had been in the courtroom.

There in the marketplace, Michael prayed aloud for his persecutors and encouraged others to pray for them as well. Finally, he prayed aloud, "Almighty eternal God, Thou who art the way and the truth, since I have not been taught other-

18   *Ibid.*, pp. 74-75.
19   *Ibid.*, p. 75.

Today, a large stone marks the likely site of Sattler's martyrdom. The stone reads "1527 Michael and Margaretha Sattler They died for their faith."

wise by anyone, so by Thy help I will testify this day to the truth and seal it with my blood."[20] Once again, he admonished the prosecutor to repentance, but the prosecutor told him to busy himself with God.

The beginning of the cruel sentence was carried out in the square, where Michael was tied to a wagon frame. It is not known if he was tied with cords or actually "forged" to the cart as the sentence ordered. To be "forged" to the cart meant that he was chained down, but not just tied with chains; a blacksmith was there to smith the chains, permanently attaching the prisoner to the wagon. Michael was then tortured with the red-hot tongs, at the square and on the way to the place of execution, and a piece of his tongue was cut out—although apparently not enough to prevent him from speaking.

Having reached the place of execution, a small bag of gunpowder was tied to Michael, designed to mercifully hasten his death. He was then thrown into the flames and the

---

20   *Ibid.*, p. 75.

powder went off, but Michael was still alive, crying out to God. When the ropes had burnt off his hands and they came free, he lifted them up, pointing with the first two fingers toward heaven—a sign that had been agreed upon before, probably signaling his faithfulness to the end. He then cried out loudly, "Father, into thy hands I commend my soul!"[21] His life ended, going to the loving Father he had served so shortly but so devotedly.

Margaretha

Left behind on this earth was Michael's wife, Margaretha. She was an attractive woman, and the Countess tried to save her life. Offering to let Margaretha live in her court, the Countess tried to entice her to recant. The effort was in vain. Margaretha—who had wished to be burned with her husband—insisted that she wanted the crown which the Lord Jesus would give her, and she wanted to keep the pledge she had given to Michael. Finally, she was led to the Neckar River, where she died a courageous death by drowning. After all their labor, suffering, and dying, Michael and Margaretha were reunited in the land of life with the Lord of the living.

---

21   *Ibid.*, p. 78.

A tiny printed copy of the Schleitheim Confession, bound with several other Anabaptist writings, from the mid-1500s.

7

A Lasting Legacy

On the evening of Monday, May 20, 1527, thin wisps of smoke rose from the small pile of ashes that was all that was left of Michael Sattler. His death—one of the most horrific which depraved and twisted human imagination can invent—would have made any future would-be Anabaptists think twice before accepting baptism, and any would-be teacher think twice before preaching or writing. To an outside observer, it could be expected that the movement would collapse. While the brilliance of his leadership could not be denied, he had only been a leader for less than a year, and now the movement was once again without him—in the same situation as it had been before he had come to prominence. Surely, the Anabaptists would once again be quarreling and would eventually come to nothing.

But Sattler's leadership left behind something which far outlasted his bodily presence. His leadership had laid the foundation for stability and faithfulness for centuries to come, and his heroic and fearless defense and martyrdom lent credibility and validity to his convictions. It is said that when a tyrant dies, his reign is over, but when a martyr dies, his reign begins. For Sattler on that May evening in 1527, his body reduced to ashes and his soul "present with the Lord," his "reign" had only begun.

The Schleitheim Confession spread rapidly in handwritten format. By July 1527, a mere five months after the confession was adopted, Ulrich Zwingli wrote that "hardly any of your people exist who have not a copy of these well founded laws, as you call them."[1] It took some time, but the Swiss Anabaptists became more and more unified around the Schleitheim Confession. Those who accepted it eventually came to be known as Swiss Brethren.

Of course, not all Anabaptists agreed with the Schleitheim Confession. Balthasar Hubmaier, who now lived in Nikolsburg, Moravia—where even the Lords of Lichtenstein had accepted rebaptism—wrote his final book, *On the Sword*, arguing that Christians may take up the sword and wage war. Not long after, while sitting in prison, he told his persecutors, "I had very great difficulties especially in the upper country with those who held that no Christian should hold governmental office or bear the sword . . . they criticized me in a public church service for holding so strongly and firmly on the sword, that a Christian may according to God's institution also bear the sword, indeed far better than an unbeliever who takes neither Christ nor his Word to heart."[2]

---

1   Ulrich Zwingli, *Refutation of the Tricks of the Catabaptists*, 1527; translation from Samuel Macauley Jackson, editor, *Selected Works of Huldreich Zwingli*, University of Pennsylvania, 1901, p. 177.
2   Balthasar Hubmaier, *Apologia*, 1528; translation from H. Wayne Pipkin & John Howard Yoder, translators and editors, *Balthasar Hubmaier: Theologian of Anabaptism*, © 1989, Herald Press (Scottdale, PA 15683), pp. 560-561. Used by permission.

Similarly, Hans Hut refused to accept the Schleitheim Confession, quarrelling about oaths with Jacob Gross and emphasizing in his trial that he was not nonresistant. He told his persecutors that

> he told the brothers . . . that they should be obedient to the government, for some imagined that Christians should not fight or go to war . . . Some also imagined that Christians should not bear weapons; indeed they made a regulation on the subject in Switzerland. He also put a stop to that and showed that this was not contrary to the divine command and not forbidden.[3]

Despite opposition, more and more Swiss Anabaptists came to embrace the faith articulated at Schleitheim. The Anabaptists' enemies were incensed.

Ulrich Zwingli

In April 1527, eight Swiss Brethren were imprisoned in the canton of Bern. Berthold Haller, a prominent Zwinglian reformer in Bern, held several discussions with them and found that he could not refute their positions with Scripture. The lodgings of the imprisoned Anabaptists were searched and a handwritten copy of the Schleitheim Confession was discovered. The Council of Bern (the governing body) asked Haller to write a refutation of the Confession. Haller did not even attempt to do so; instead, he sent the copy to Ulrich Zwingli and asked him to refute it.

In the meantime, in Zürich, copies of the Confession were piling up on Zwingli's desk. He had already received his first copy from the Zwinglian reformer Johannes Oecalampadius. Before long, he had four copies of the Confession. He undertook the task of refuting it in his final book

---

3   Hans Hut, trial statements, 1527; translation from James M. Stayer, *Anabaptists and the Sword*, 1972, Coronado Press, pp. 158-159.

Printing in the Sixteenth Century

"Printing is the latest of God's gifts and the greatest," Martin Luther said. "Through printing God wills to make the cause of true religion known to the whole world even to the ends of the earth."[1]

The process of printing in the sixteenth century began with Gutenberg's revolutionary invention, movable type. Printers kept supplies of the tiny metal letters, which they arranged into words and sentences in frames, exactly as they would appear in print (but backward, so that it would print correctly). The frames were then placed into the printing press and ink was applied to the type. Paper was placed on the type and the press lowered, applying pressure to the paper and forcing it to absorb the ink on the raised letters. When the press was lifted, the paper was removed and allowed to dry.

While vastly more efficient than copying manuscripts by hand, printing required a lot of materials and laborers. To print forbidden material, such as Anabaptist writings, was very risky.

Not only did the shop owner have to be an Anabaptist or a thoroughly trustworthy sympathizer, everyone who worked on the project would have to be as well. Furthermore, the project had to be kept completely secret; even a stray customer wandering

---

1   As cited by Gregory B. Graybill, *The Honeycomb Scroll*, 2015, Fortress Press, p. 50.

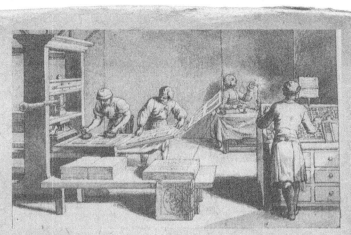

This illustration from 1770 shows a worker on the left inking the type, the one next to him removing a printed page, one working at the table (perhaps editing), and the one on the right setting type.

into the shop could see the forbidden materials and inform on the print shop, putting lives and livelihoods at risk. Once printed, the pages had to be stored. Then they had to be distributed, as they had not been printed simply to sit unread in the printer's basement. All this took a network of committed people willing to run risks for the sake of God's kingdom. With all the risks, it is amazing that so many Anabaptist books were printed in the sixteenth century.

against the Anabaptists, named *Refutation of the Tricks of the Catabaptists.*

Zwingli knew that he did not want to spread the beliefs of the Anabaptists by publishing the German text of the Schleitheim Confession, so he translated the text into Latin and wrote his book in Latin, for the educated clergy of Switzerland. Ironically, the first time the Schleitheim Confession was ever printed was by the Protestant Reformers!

The *Refutation* was written in three parts. Part 2 deals with the Schleitheim Confession. Zwingli calls the Confession "the grounds of your superstition" and says that even though they have never been printed, "hardly any of your people exist who have not a copy of these well founded laws, as you call them." Zwingli goes on to accuse the Anabaptists: "Why, pray, do you not publish what are so divine and so salutary? But counsels evilly conceived fear the light, and are terrified at the judgment of learned and pious men. For this reason you do not publish the dogmas, articles, principles of your superstition."[4] Of course, the Anabaptists were a persecuted minority group

Ulrich Zwingli wrote against the Schleitheim Confession.

4   Ulrich Zwingli, *Refutation of the Tricks of the Catabaptists*, 1527; translation from Samuel Macauley Jackson, editor, *Selected Works of Huldreich Zwingli*, University of Pennsylvania, 1901, p. 177.

whose access to the printing press depended on finding a printer who was willing to risk his life to publish their writings. Zwingli was being unreasonable and intellectually dishonest.

Zwingli called the Anabaptists' beliefs outlined in the Confession "fanatical, foolish, bold, impudent," then added, "This is not too severe." He continued to smear the Anabaptists, saying that the second article on excommunication "is all so crude that it smells of nothing but a three days' theologian" (someone who has been a theologian for only three days). He called nonresistance "a kind of womanish gentleness." The many names he called the Anabaptists in this book include "monsters of deceit," the "heretical church of the rebaptized," "stupid seducers," and "vain seducers of old women."

The Confession Printed

Additional literature was soon produced and circulated along with the Schleitheim Confession. In particular, Wilhelm Reublin wrote an account of Michael Sattler's trial and martyrdom, as did two others. These accounts of Michael's martyrdom were so popular that the Austrian government, which sentenced Sattler, wanted to write a counter-booklet, but concluded that it would be of no use.

In 1533—perhaps earlier—the Brethren were able to print the Schleitheim Confession in German for the first time, along with Sattler's letter to Horb, an account of Sattler's martyrdom, and a tract on divorce. Another printing, lacking the divorce tract, was printed about the same time. It is not known whether it was older or newer than the 1533 edition because it is undated. The Confession was also reprinted sometime in the mid-1500s and again in 1686.

In addition to being read and reprinted, the Swiss Brethren continued to use the arguments of the Schleitheim Confession, sometimes expanding on them and other times repeating them almost verbatim. In 1572, following the printing of the minutes from the Frankenthal Disputation (1571) between Anabaptists and Reformed, some Swiss Anabaptists compiled a reply, titled *A Short, Simple Confession.* It drew on several earlier Anabaptist works, including the Schleitheim Confession. The *Simple Confession*'s article on the sword seems to draw on the Schleitheim Confession;[5] its article on the oath contains much material drawn directly, with slight modifications, from the Schleitheim Confession.[6] Earlier, about 1557, Swiss Brethren martyr Thomas von Imbroich wrote to his fellow-believers from prison to "Beware of false brethren, and keep yourselves clear of them in accord with our Agreement, and do not grow weary therein"[7]—an apparent reference to the Schleitheim Confession.

Around 1543, some Anabaptists had the Schleitheim Confession, the account of Michael Sattler's martyrdom, and possibly some of the other Sattler-related materials translated into French. They had 1,500 copies printed in the German-speaking part of Switzerland for distribution in the French-speaking parts of Switzerland. A copy fell into the hands of William Farel, a Protestant reformer, who forwarded it to John Calvin with the request that he write a refutation.

---

5   See, for instance, the statement that Jesus "fled" when the people wanted to make Him king, followed by citing Romans 8:29, one of the Scriptures which the Schleitheim Confession quotes after the same account from Jesus' ministry. *A Short, Simple Confession*, 1572; translation from C. Arnold Snyder, *Later Writings of the Swiss Anabaptists 1529-1592*, 2017, Pandora Press, pp. 282-283.

6   *A Short, Simple Confession*, 1572; translation from C. Arnold Snyder, *Later Writings of the Swiss Anabaptists 1529-1592*, 2017, Pandora Press, pp. 303-304.

7   Thomas von Imbroich, Sixth Epistle, c. 1557; translation from Leonard Gross (editor), *Golden Apples in Silver Bowls*, 1999, Lancaster Mennonite Historical Society, p. 133.

John Calvin versus Schleitheim

Calvin's refutation, published in French in 1544 and in English in 1549, was titled *A Short Instruction for to arme all good Christian people agaynst the pestiferous errours of the common secte of the Anabaptistes.* He began by saying that the Confession book was "unworthy to be spoken of,

or to be made mention of," and saying that he could "occupy myself, as men think, in better things." He apologized for writing a refutation of "a thing so barren and trifling, as is this little book, which appeareth to be made by ignorant people." He said it "hath no need of resolution towards them that have learning and understanding . . . in that it is so unlearnedly

John Calvin wrote against the Schleitheim Confession, saying it was "unlearnedly & foolishly written."

& foolishly written." Nevertheless, he stated that the book had been sent to him "from far countries" by "many good faithful men," who asked him to refute it, "with testimony that it was very needful for the health of many souls, that I should take it in hand." So he attempted "to shew unto all faithful Christian men which be rude and unlearned, what and how dangerous a poison this doctrine of the Anabaptists is: and also arm them by the word of God against the same, to the end that they be not deceived."

While Calvin wrote in a much more restrained manner than Zwingli, he still called the Anabaptists a long list of names, including "ignorant people," "poor fantasticals," "poor beasts," "dull-heads," "mad bedlams," "brainless men," "hogs," "beasts," and "mad men."

Beyond the Swiss

Michael Sattler's influence, and that of the Schleitheim Confession, soon reached far beyond the Swiss Brethren. The Hutterites, the communal Anabaptists of Moravia, also valued the Schleitheim Confession and honored Michael Sattler, whose memory was enshrined in their *Great Chronicle*, receiving nothing but praise. In fact, the *Chronicle* remembers him as being more learned and capable than he was in real life, making him into "a scholar in Hebrew and Latin."[8] The Hutterites copied the Schleitheim Confession in their handwritten collections of spiritual writings.[9]

But they did more than just copy it—they incorporated it into some of their own materials. For instance, in 1557, the Hutterites wrote a book responding to a work against the Anabaptists by the Lutheran theologian Philip Melanchthon. The Hutterites' response on the topic of the sword included distinct echoes of the Schleitheim Confession's article on the sword. Their article on the oath utilized, nearly word-for-word, much of Schleitheim's discussion on the oath.[10]

Another example is related to a famous story of Hutterite prisoners. On St. Nicholas Day (December 6), 1539, over 100 Hutterites and other Anabaptists—including some Swiss Brethren—were arrested in Steinabrunn, Austria, and imprisoned in Falkenstein Castle. When they refused to recant or give up community life, the men were sentenced to

---

8   While he surely knew Latin, it is highly doubtful that Sattler knew Hebrew. *The Chronicle of the Hutterian Brethren Volume I*, 1987, Plough Publishing House, p. 51.

9   Robert Friedmann, "The Schleitheim Confession (1527) and Other Doctrinal Writings of the Swiss Brethren in a Hitherto Unknown Edition," *Mennonite Quarterly Review* 16(2) (April 1942):82-98, p. 86.

10   *The Defense Against the Process at Worms on the Rhine*, 1557; translated by Henry Walter, 2017, pp. 26, 41-46.

St. Nicholas's Day

By the sixteenth century, the Catholic Church had made so many days of remembrance for various saints that most days could be designated as either a saint's day or by its relationship to a saint's day (i.e., the Tuesday after St. Nicholas's Day). For instance, the Schleitheim Confession was adopted on St. Matthias's Day (February 24).

The Hutterites at Steinabrunn were arrested on St. Nicholas's Day, December 6. The legends surrounding Nicholas of Myra eventually grew into today's worldwide myth of "Santa Claus."

In the Middle Ages, St. Nicholas was known as patron saint of sailors, barrel-makers, picklers, florists, etc.—and children. In the twelfth century, he began to be imagined as the deliverer of gifts on the eve of his own feast day, December 6. In the nineteenth century in the United States, as part of an American re-imagination of Christmas traditions, St. Nicholas received the new form of his name, "Santa Claus" (from the Dutch Sinterklaas) and his gift-bearing visit was moved from the night of December 5 to that of December 24. In 1863, during the height of the Civil War, Thomas Nast of *Harper's Weekly* gave the world the picture of the round, bearded, jolly man who would be imagined the world over as Santa Claus.

Thomas Nast imagined a round, bearded Santa Claus giving gifts to Union soldiers during the Civil War.

be galley slaves and were chained together and marched to Triest, on the Adriatic Sea. Preserved by the Hutterites is a confession of faith associated with the prisoners. While some sources imply that it was written by the prisoners themselves, it may have been written by the Hutterite leaders on behalf of the prisoners. This confession incorporates all of Articles 3 (Lord's Supper) and 6 (sword) and parts of 4 (separation) and 7 (oaths) from the Schleitheim Confession. If it was indeed written by the prisoners, perhaps one of them possessed a small printed copy of the Schleitheim Confession, like that in the Mennonite Historical Library in Goshen, Indiana (pictured at the beginning of the chapter).

Dutch translations of the Schleitheim Confession (along with the Letter to Horb and the account of Sattler's trial and martyrdom) were printed in 1560 and 1565. Michael Sattler was one of only two non-Dutch martyrs (the other being Stephen) honored by inclusion in the original Dutch Mennonite martyr book, *Het Offer des Heeren* (*The Offering of the Lord*). This book was continually reprinted and expanded until it became the *Martyrs Mirror*, which includes a lengthy account of Sattler's martyrdom as well as his Letter to Horb.

Sattler's Legacy

Contrary to what his enemies wished and what men might have expected, Michael Sattler's death did not end his legacy or his influence. With heroic faith and courage, Michael Sattler was willing to serve God and follow Christ no matter the cost; thus, God was able to use him as an instrument to bring stability and a common core of Scriptural understandings which has survived the centuries. Sattler's legacy of courage, conviction, and faith, the Schleitheim Confession which he was instrumental in helping to produce, and the union represented by the Confession which he helped bring about, helped to unite the Swiss Anabaptist movement around a Scriptural vision which has helped to guide and direct it ever since. Furthermore, this vision also impacted other branches of Anabaptism, helping to give vision and direction to them as well. In the following centuries, the Schleitheim Confession and Michael Sattler's writings have continued to be influential, but more significantly, Schleitheim's two-kingdom foundation endured to shape the worldview of the Swiss Brethren and thousands of Anabaptists since. Both in the convictions it articulated and the concepts it promoted, the Schleitheim Confession gave definition to the movement which produced it, and defines the continuing descendants of that movement to this very day.

Michael Sattler's noble example challenges us today to follow Christ with the same gelassenheit, passion, and Scriptural conviction that he did.

Part 2

The Writings of Michael Sattler

Document 1
Letter to Capito and Bucer

This is Michael Sattler's earliest known writing. It was a letter to his friends, the Protestant reformers Wolfgang Capito and Martin Bucer, explaining why he was leaving Strasbourg and why he could not agree with their rejection of radical obedience to New Testament commands. Translation from *The Legacy of Michael Sattler*, trans. and ed. by John H. Yoder, pp. 21-24. Copyright © 1973 by Herald Press, Scottdale, PA 15683. Used by permission.

Michael Sattler to his beloved brothers in God Capito and Bucer and others who love and confess Christ from the heart.

Grace and peace from God our Father through Jesus Christ our Savior. Dear brothers in God! As I recently spoke with you in brotherly moderation and friendliness on several points, which I together with my brothers and sisters have understood out of Scripture, namely out of the New Testament, and you for your part as the ones asked answered in similar moderation and friendliness as follows: Paul writes in 1 Timothy 1 that love is the end of the commandment, wherefore it is necessary that all of the commands of God be guided by the same—I am not able so to conceive, in my understanding and conscience, that this may be done as you do it with every point; namely with baptism, the Lord's Supper, force or the sword, the oath, the ban, and all the commandments of God. What hinders me is the following:

1. Christ came to save all of those who would believe in Him alone.
2. He who believes and is baptized will be saved; he who does not believe will be damned.
3. Faith in Jesus Christ reconciles us with the Father and gives us access to Him.
4. Baptism incorporates all believers into the body of Christ, of which He is the head.
5. Christ is the head of His body, i.e., of the believers or the congregation.
6. As the head is minded, so must its members also be.
7. The foreknown and called believers shall be conformed to the image of Christ.
8. Christ is despised in the world. So are also those who are His; He has no kingdom in the world, but that which is of this world is against His kingdom.
9. Believers are chosen out of the world, therefore the world hates them.
10. The devil is prince over the whole world, in whom all the children of darkness rule.
11. Christ is Prince of the Spirit, in whom all who walk in the light live.
12. The devil seeks to destroy, Christ seeks to save.
13. The flesh is against the spirit and the spirit against the flesh.

14. Those who are spiritual are Christ's; those who are carnal belong to death and to the wrath of God.
15. Christians are fully yielded and have placed their trust in their Father in heaven without any outward or worldly arms.
16. The citizenship of Christians is in heaven and not on earth.
17. Christians are the members of the household of God and fellow citizens of the saints, and not of the world.
18. But they are the true Christians who practice in deed the teaching of Christ.
19. Flesh and blood, pomp and temporal, earthly honor and the world cannot comprehend the kingdom of Christ.
20. In sum: There is nothing in common between Christ and Belial.

Such considerations, and still much more of the same kind, which do not now come to mind, hinder me, dear brothers, from understanding your general assertion on every subject which you advocate with the words of Paul cited above. Therefore, my beloved in God, I know of no comfort in all despair except to address an humble prayer to God the Father for you and for me, that He might be willing to teach us in all truth by His Spirit. Herewith I commend you to the Lord, for as I understand it, I can no longer remain here without doing a special dishonor to God; therefore I must for the sake of my conscience leave the field to the opposition. I beg you herein, that you understand this as an act of Christian humility on my part. The Lord will ultimately dispose.

Be mercifully considerate, I pray you, of those who are in prison and do not permit a merciful judgment to be superseded by a blind, spiteful, and cruel one. Those who are in error (if that they were) are not to be coerced but after a second admonition to be avoided. Christians admonish benevolently, out of sympathy and compassion for the sinful, and do not legalistically coerce persons this way or that. May the Lord God have mercy on us all and give us His Spirit to lead us in the way, Christ Jesus, through whom we can again come into our kingdom, fatherland, and citizenship. Amen. The Lord be with you all dear brothers in God. Amen.

Michael Sattler, your brother in God the heavenly Father.

Document 2
The Schleitheim Confession

Translation from John C. Wenger, "The Schleitheim Confession of Faith," *Mennonite Quarterly Review* 19(4) (October 1945):243-253. Used by permission.

May joy, peace and mercy from our Father through the atonement[1] of the blood of Christ Jesus, together with the gifts of the Spirit—Who is sent from the Father to all believers for their strength and comfort and for their perseverance in all tribulation until the end, Amen—be to all those who love God, who are the children of light, and who are scattered everywhere as it has been ordained of God our Father, where they

---

1   The German word here translated "atonement" is *vereynigung*, a form of which (*vereinigt*) is used repeatedly throughout the Articles in reference to the unity or agreement of the Anabaptists at Schleitheim. Here it seems to mean that the blood of Jesus Christ has brought the Anabaptists into unity. (Personal communication, Urs Leu via Dale Burkholder.)

are with one mind assembled together in one God and Father of us all: Grace and peace of heart be with you all, Amen.

Beloved brethren and sisters in the Lord: First and supremely we are always concerned for your consolation and the assurance of your conscience (which was previously misled) so that you may not always remain foreigners to us and by right almost completely excluded, but that you may turn again to the true implanted members of Christ, who have been armed through patience and knowledge of themselves, and have therefore again been united with us in the strength of a godly Christian spirit and zeal for God.

It is also apparent with what cunning the devil has turned us aside, so that he might destroy and bring to an end the work of God which in mercy and grace has been partly begun in us. But Christ, the true Shepherd of our souls, Who has begun this in us, will certainly direct the same and teach [us] to His honor and our salvation, Amen.

Dear brethren and sisters, we who have been assembled in the Lord at Schleitheim on the Border, make known in points and articles to all who love God that as concerns us we are of one mind to abide in the Lord as God's obedient children, [His] sons and daughters, we who have been and shall be separated from the world in everything, [and] completely at peace. To God alone be praise and glory without the contradiction of any brethren. In this we have perceived the oneness of the Spirit of our Father and of our common Christ with us. For the Lord is the Lord of peace and not of quarreling, as Paul points out. That you may understand in what articles this has been formulated you should observe and note [the following].

A very great offense has been introduced by certain false brethren among us, so that some have turned aside from the faith, in the way they intend to practice and observe the freedom of the Spirit and of Christ. But such have missed the truth and to their condemnation are given over to the lasciviousness and self-indulgence of the flesh. They think faith and love may do and permit everything, and nothing will harm them nor condemn them, since they are believers.

Observe, you who are God's members in Christ Jesus, that faith in the Heavenly Father through Jesus Christ does not take such form. It does not produce and result in such things as these false brethren and sisters do and teach. Guard yourselves and be warned of such people, for they do not serve our Father, but their father, the devil.

But you are not that way. For they that are Christ's have crucified the flesh with its passions and lusts. You understand me well and [know] the brethren whom we mean. Separate yourselves from them for they are perverted. Petition the Lord that they may have the knowledge which leads to repentance, and [pray] for us that we may have constancy to persevere in the way which we have espoused, for the honor of God and of Christ, His Son, Amen.

The articles which we discussed and on which we were of one mind are these 1. Baptism; 2. The Ban [Excommunication]; 3. Breaking of Bread; 4. Separation from the Abomination; 5. Pastors in the Church; 6. The Sword; and 7. The Oath.

First. Observe concerning baptism: Baptism shall be given to all those who have learned repentance and amendment of life, and who believe truly that their sins are taken away by Christ, and to all those who walk in the resurrection of Jesus Christ, and wish to be buried with Him in death, so that they may be resurrected with Him, and to all those who with this significance request it [baptism] of us and demand it for themselves. This excludes all infant baptism, the highest and chief abomination of the pope. In this you have the foundation and testimony of the apostles. Mt. 28, Mk. 16, Acts 2, 8, 16, 19. This we wish to hold simply, yet firmly and with assurance.

Second. We are agreed as follows on the ban: The ban shall be employed with all those who have given themselves to the Lord, to walk in His commandments, and with all those who are baptized into the one body of Christ and who are called brethren or sisters, and yet who slip sometimes and fall into error and sin, being inadvertently overtaken. The same shall be admonished twice in secret and the third time openly disciplined or banned according to the command of Christ. Mt. 18. But this shall be done according to the regulation of the Spirit (Mt. 5) before the breaking of bread, so that we may break and eat one bread, with one mind and in one love, and may drink of one cup.

Third. In the breaking of bread we are of one mind and are agreed [as follows]: All those who wish to break one bread in remembrance of the broken body of Christ, and all who wish to drink of one drink as a remembrance of the shed blood of Christ, shall be united beforehand by baptism in one body of Christ which is the church of God and whose Head is Christ. For as Paul points out we cannot at the same time be partakers of the Lord's table and the table of devils; we cannot at the same time drink the cup of the Lord and the cup of the devil. That is, all those who have fellowship with the dead works of darkness have no part in the light. Therefore all who follow the devil and the world have no part with those who are called unto God out of the world. All who lie in evil have no part in the good.

Therefore it is and must be [thus]: Whoever has not been called by one God to one faith, to one baptism, to one Spirit, to one body, with all the children of God's church, cannot be made [into] one bread with them, as indeed must be done if one is truly to break bread according to the command of Christ.

Fourth. We are agreed [as follows] on separation: A separation shall be made from the evil and from the wickedness which the devil planted in the world; in this manner, simply that we shall not have fellowship with them [the wicked] and not run with them in the multitude of their abominations. This is the way it is: Since all who do not walk in the obedience of faith, and have not united themselves with God so that they wish to do His will, are a great abomination before God, it is not possible for anything to grow or issue from them except abominable things. For truly all creatures are in but two classes, good and bad, believing and unbelieving, darkness and light, the world and those who [have come] out of the world, God's temple and idols, Christ and Belial; and none can have part with the other.

To us then the command of the Lord is clear when He calls upon us to be separate from the evil and thus He will be our God and we shall be His sons and daughters.

He further admonishes us to withdraw from Babylon and the earthly Egypt that we may not be partakers of the pain and suffering which the Lord will bring upon them.

From all this we should learn that everything which is not united with our God and Christ cannot be other than an abomination which we should shun and flee from. By this is meant all popish and antipopish works and church services, meetings and church attendance, drinking houses, civic affairs, the commitments [made in] unbelief and other things of that kind, which are highly regarded by the world and yet are carried on in flat contradiction to the command of God, in accordance with all the unrighteousness which is in the world. From all these things we shall be separated and have no part with them for they are nothing but an abomination, and they are the cause of our being hated before our Christ Jesus, Who has set us free from the slavery of the flesh and fitted us for the service of God through the Spirit Whom He has given us.

Therefore there will also unquestionably fall from us the unchristian, devilish weapons of force—such as sword, armor and the like, and all their use [either] for friends or against one's enemies—by virtue of the word of Christ, Resist not [him that is] evil.

Fifth. We are agreed as follows on pastors in the church of God: The pastor in the church of God shall, as Paul has prescribed, be one who out-and-out has a good report of those who are outside the faith. This office shall be to read, to admonish and teach, to warn, to discipline, to ban in the church, to lead out in prayer for the advancement of all the brethren and sisters, to lift up the bread when it is to be broken, and in all things to see to the care of the body of Christ, in order that it may be built up and developed, and the mouth of the slanderer be stopped.

This one moreover shall be supported of the church which has chosen him, wherein he may be in need, so that he who serves the Gospel may live of the Gospel as the Lord has ordained. But if a pastor should do something requiring discipline, he shall not be dealt with except [on the testimony of] two or three witnesses. And when they sin they shall be disciplined before all in order that the others may fear.

But should it happen that through the cross this pastor should be banished or led to the Lord [through martyrdom] another shall be ordained in his place in the same hour so that God's little flock and people may not be destroyed.

Sixth. We are agreed as follows concerning the sword: The sword is ordained of God outside the perfection of Christ. It punishes and puts to death the wicked, and guards and protects the good. In the Law the sword was ordained for the punishment of the wicked and for their death, and the same [sword] is [now] ordained to be used by the worldly magistrates.

In the perfection of Christ, however, only the ban is used for a warning and for the excommunication of the one who has sinned, without putting the flesh to death,—simply the warning and the command to sin no more.

Now it will be asked by many who do not recognize [this as] the will of Christ for us, whether a Christian may or should employ the sword against the wicked for the defense and protection of the good, or for the sake of love.

Our reply is unanimously as follows: Christ teaches and commands us to learn of Him, for He is meek and lowly in heart and so shall we find rest to our souls. Also Christ says to the heathenish woman who was taken in adultery, not that one should stone her according to the law of His Father (and yet He says, As the Father has commanded me, thus I do), but in mercy and forgiveness and warning, to sin no more. Such [an attitude] we also ought to take completely according to the rule of the ban.

Secondly, it will be asked concerning the sword, whether a Christian shall pass sentence in worldly dispute and strife such as unbelievers have with one another. This is our united answer: Christ did not wish to decide or pass judgment between brother and brother in the case of the inheritance, but refused to do so. Therefore we should do likewise.

Thirdly, it will be asked concerning the sword, Shall one be a magistrate if one should be chosen as such? The answer is as follows: They wished to make Christ king, but He fled and did not view it as the arrangement of His Father. Thus shall we do as He did, and follow Him, and so shall we not walk in darkness. For He Himself says, He who wishes to come after me, let him deny himself and take up his cross and follow me. Also, He Himself forbids the [employment of] the force of the sword saying, The worldly princes lord it over them, etc., but not so shall it be with you. Further, Paul says, Whom God did foreknow He also did predestinate to be conformed to the image of His Son, etc. Also Peter says, Christ has suffered (not ruled) and left us an example, that ye should follow His steps.

Finally it will be observed that it is not appropriate for a Christian to serve as a magistrate because of these points:

The government magistracy is according to the flesh, but the Christians' is according to the Spirit; their houses and dwelling remain in this world, but the Christians' are in heaven; their citizenship is in this world, but the Christians' citizenship is in heaven; the weapons of their conflict and war are carnal and against the flesh only, but the Christians' weapons are spiritual, against the fortification of the devil. The worldlings are armed with steel and iron, but the Christians are armed with the armor of God, with truth, righteousness, peace, faith, salvation and the Word of God. In brief, as is the mind of Christ toward us, so shall the mind of the members of the body of Christ be through Him in all things, that there may be no schism in the body through which it would be destroyed. For every kingdom divided against itself will be destroyed. Now since Christ is as it is written of Him, His members must also be the same, that His body may remain complete and united to its own advancement and upbuilding.

Seventh. We are agreed as follows concerning the oath: The oath is a confirmation among those who are quarreling or making promises. In the Law it is commanded to be performed in God's Name, but only in truth, not falsely. Christ, who teaches the perfection of the Law, prohibits all swearing to His [followers], whether true or false,—neither by heaven, nor by the earth, nor by Jerusalem, nor by our head,—and that for the reason which He shortly thereafter gives, For you are not able to make one hair white or black. So you see it is for this reason that all swearing is forbidden: we cannot fulfill that which we promise when we swear, for we cannot change [even] the very least thing on us.

Now there are some who do not give credence to the simple command of God, but object with this question: Well now, did not God swear to Abraham by Himself (since He was God) when He promised him that He would be with him and that He would be his God if he would keep His commandments,—why then should I not also swear when

I promise to someone? Answer: Hear what the Scripture says: God, since He wished more abundantly to show unto the heirs the immutability of His counsel, inserted an oath, that by two immutable things (in which it is impossible for God to lie) we might have a strong consolation. Observe the meaning of this Scripture: What God forbids you to do, He has power to do, for everything is possible for Him. God swore an oath to Abraham, says the Scripture, so that He might show that His counsel is immutable. That is, no one can withstand nor thwart His will; therefore He can keep His oath. But we can do nothing, as is said above by Christ, to keep or perform [our oaths]: therefore we shall not swear at all.

Then others further say as follows: It is not forbidden of God to swear in the New Testament, when it is actually commanded in the Old, but it is forbidden only to swear by heaven, earth, Jerusalem and our head. Answer: Hear the Scripture, He who swears by heaven swears by God's throne and by Him who sitteth thereon. Observe: it is forbidden to swear by heaven, which is only the throne of God: how much more is it forbidden [to swear] by God Himself! Ye fools and blind, which is greater, the throne or Him that sitteth thereon?

Further some say, Because evil is now [in the world, and] because man needs God for [the establishment of] the truth, so did the apostles Peter and Paul also swear. Answer: Peter and Paul only testify of that which God promised to Abraham with the oath. They themselves promise nothing, as the example indicates clearly. Testifying and swearing are two different things. For when a person swears he is in the first place promising future things, as Christ was promised to Abraham Whom we a long time afterwards received. But when a person bears testimony he is testifying about the present, whether it is good or evil, as Simeon spoke to Mary about Christ and testified, Behold this (child) is set for the fall and rising of many in Israel, and for a sign which shall be spoken against.

Christ also taught us along the same line when He said, Let your communication be Yea, yea; Nay, nay; for whatsoever is more than these cometh of evil. He says, Your speech or word shall be yea and nay. (However) when one does not wish to understand, he remains closed to the meaning. Christ is simply Yea and Nay, and all those who seek Him simply will understand His Word. Amen.

Dear brethren and sisters in the Lord: These are the articles of certain brethren who had heretofore been in error and who had failed to agree in the true understanding, so that many weaker consciences were perplexed, causing the Name of God to be greatly slandered. Therefore there has been a great need for us to become of one mind in the Lord, which has come to pass. To God be praise and glory!

Now since you have so well understood the will of God which has been made known by us, it will be necessary for you to achieve perseveringly, without interruption, the known will of God. For you know well what the servant who sinned knowingly heard as his recompense.

Everything which you have unwittingly done and confessed as evil doing is forgiven you through the believing prayer which is offered by us in our meeting for all our shortcomings and guilt. [This state is yours] through the gracious forgiveness of God and through the blood of Jesus Christ. Amen.

Keep watch on all who do not walk according to the simplicity of the divine truth which is stated in this letter from [the decisions of] our meeting, so that everyone among us will be governed by the rule of the ban and henceforth the entry of false brethren and sisters among us may be prevented.

Eliminate from you that which is evil and the Lord will be your God and you will be His sons and daughters.

Dear brethren, keep in mind what Paul admonishes Timothy when he says, The grace of God that bringeth salvation hath appeared to all men, teaching us that, denying ungodliness and worldly lusts, we should live soberly, righteously, and godly, in this present world; looking for that blessed hope, and the glorious appearing of the great God and our Saviour Jesus Christ; Who gave Himself for us, that He might redeem us from all iniquity, and purify unto Himself a people of His own, zealous of good works. Think on this and exercise yourselves therein and the God of peace will be with you.

May the Name of God be hallowed eternally and highly praised, Amen. May the Lord give you His peace, Amen.

The Acts of Schleitheim on the Border [Canton Schaffhausen, Switzerland], on Matthias' [Day] [February 24], Anno MDXXVII [1527].

Document 3

Farewell Letter to the Church at Horb

Written by Michael Sattler while imprisoned in the tower at Binsdorf. From *The Legacy of Michael Sattler*, trans. and ed. by John H. Yoder, pp. 55-63. Copyright © 1973 by Herald Press, Scottdale, PA 15683. Used by permission.

To the Church of God at Horb, My Beloved Brothers and Sisters in the Lord

May grace and mercy from God the heavenly Father through Jesus Christ our Lord, and the power of Their Spirit, be with you, brothers and sisters, beloved of God. I cannot forget you although I am not present in the body, but constantly am in care and watching over you as my fellow members, so that not one might ever be drawn away and robbed from the body, whereby the entire body with all its members would be saddened, especially now, as the fury of the tearing wolf has risen most high and has become most powerful, so that he also challenged me to fight with him; but to God be eternally the praise, his head has been split greatly, I hope, his entire body will soon no longer be, as stands written in 4 Esdras 11.[1]

Dear brothers and sisters, you know with what zeal and love I admonished you recently when I was with you, that you would be sincere and righteous in all patience and love of God, so that you can be recognized in the midst of this adulterous generation of godless men, like bright and shining lights which God the heavenly Father has kindled with the knowledge of Him and the light of the Spirit. With that same zeal I now pray and exhort you, that you might walk surely and circumspectly toward those who are without as unbelievers, so that in no way our office which God has laid upon us might be shamed or justifiably mocked. Remember the Lord who gave you a coin (for he will again require the same with interest), lest that one talent be taken away from you. Place it at interest according to the command of the Lord who entrusted it to you. I testify to you by the grace of God that you are valiant and that you walk as befits and becomes the saints of God. Give heed how the Lord rewards lazy servants, namely the lazy and tired hearts, clumsy and cold in the love of God and the brothers; you have experienced what I write you.

Let this be a warning to you lest you receive the same punishment from God. Guard, guard yourselves against such, so that you do not also learn their abominations, who act against the command and law of God, but admonish the same with strict attentiveness and excommunication according to the command of Christ, yet with all love and compassion for their coldness of heart. If you do this, you will soon see where among the wolves the sheep of God dwell, and will see a quick and rapid separation of those who do not wish to walk the surefooted and living way of Christ, namely

---

1   A reference to the Old Testament Apocrypha.

through cross, misery, imprisonment, self-denial, and finally through death; thereby you can assuredly present yourselves to God your heavenly Father as a purely righteous, upright congregation of Christ, purified through His blood, that she might be holy and irreproachable before God and men, separated and purified from all idolatry and abomination, so that the Lord of all lords might dwell among them and [that she might] be a tabernacle to Him.

Dear brothers, note what I write, whether it is of the Lord, and apply yourselves to walk accordingly. Let no one shift your goal, as has hitherto happened to some, but go right on, firm and undeviating, in all patience, that you might not of yourselves make void and set aside the cross which God has laid upon you, which would be counter to the honor and praise of God, and furthermore would break and dissolve His eternal, veritable, righteous and life-giving commandments.

Be not weary if you are chastised by the Lord, for he whom God loves He chastises and, like a father, He finds pleasure in His son. What would you undertake if you sought to flee from God? What could help you to escape from Him? Is not God the one who fills heaven and earth? Does He not know every secret of your vain heart and the wantonness of your reins? All that is, is manifest before Him, and nothing is hid from Him. You vain man, where would you flee that God would not see you? Why do you flee the rod of your Father? If you will not be drawn according to the will of your Father, you cannot be an heir to His possessions: why do you prefer a brief and passing rest to the blessed, measured chastisement and discipline (for your salvation) of the Lord? How long will you eat meat from the fatness of Egypt? How long will you be carnally minded? Flesh passes away and all of its glory, only the Word of the Lord remains eternally.

Dear brothers, note what I write you, for it is needful to you, for you see that there are few who are willing to persevere in the chastisement of the Lord, whereas the majority when they suffer something minor in the flesh, become dull and slack, and no more look upon the Prince of our faith and its perfecter Jesus. So they forget all His commandments and cease to treasure the jewel which the calling of God holds out up above and points to for those who conquer, but rather consider much more valuable and useful this temporal ease which they can see, to the eternal which one must hope for.

There are some, where this is put up to them, who blame God, though most wrongly, as if He were not willing to keep them in His protection. You know whom I mean. Watch out that you do not be partakers with such.

Further, dear fellow members in Christ, you should be admonished not to forget love, without which it is not possible that you be a Christian congregation. You know what love is through the testimony of Paul our fellow brother; he says: Love is patient and kind, not jealous, not puffed up, not ambitious, seeks not its own, thinks no evil, rejoices not in iniquity, rejoices in the truth, suffers everything, endures everything, believes everything, hopes everything. If you understand this text, you will find the love of God and of neighbor. If you love God you will rejoice in the truth and will believe, hope, and endure everything that comes from God. Thereby the shortcomings mentioned above can be removed and avoided. But if you love the neighbor, you will not scold or ban zealously, will not seek your own, will not remember evil, will not be ambitious or puffed up, but kind, righteous, generous in all gifts, humble and sympathetic with the weak and imperfect.

Some brothers, I know who they are, have fallen short of this love. They have not wanted to build up one another in love, but are puffed up and have become useless with vain speculation and understanding of those things which God wants to keep secret to Himself. I do not admonish or reject the grace and revelation of God, but the inflated use of this revelation. What is the use, says Paul, if one speaks with all sorts of tongues of men and angels? And knows all mysteries, wisdom, and has all faith, he says, what is all that worth if the one and only love is not exercised? You have experienced what such puffed up speech and unwisdom have brought to birth. You still see daily their false fruits, whether they have abandoned themselves completely to God.

Let no one shift your goal, which has been set in the letter of the Holy Scripture, which is sealed by the blood of Christ and of many witnesses of Jesus. Do not listen what they say from their father, for he is a deceiver, believe not their spirit, for it is completely submerged in the flesh. Judge what I write you, take the matter to heart, so that this abomination may be separated from you and you might be found to be the humble, fruitful, and obedient children of God.

Brothers, wonder not that I deal with the matter thus seriously, for it does not happen without a reason. You have probably learned from brothers how some of ours have been taken prisoner and then, when the brothers had also been taken prisoner in Horb, how we were taken to Binsdorf. During this time we underwent all sorts of attacks from the adversaries. They menaced us once with a cord, then with fire, then with the sword. In such dangers I completely abandoned myself to the Lord in His will and readied myself for death for the sake of His testimony, with all my brothers and my wife. Then I thought of the great number of false brothers and of you who are so few, yea, such a small band; and how few faithful workers there are in the vineyard of the Lord. So it seemed needful to me to urge you by this exhortation to follow us in God's combat and thereby to console you that you might not become weary under the discipline of the Lord.

In sum: dear brothers and sisters, this letter shall be my farewell from all of you who truly love and follow God (I do not know the others), and a testimony of my love toward you, which God has put in my heart for the sake of your salvation. I would have desired, and, I might hope, it would have been useful, that I had been able to continue for a little time longer to work at the Lord's task, but it is better for my sake to be released and with Christ to await the hope of the blessed. The Lord can certainly raise up for Himself another laborer to complete His work. Pray that reapers may be driven out into the harvest, for the time of threshing has come near. The abomination of desolation is visible among you. The elect servants and maidservants of God will be marked on the forehead with the name of their Father. The world has arisen against those who are redeemed from its error. The gospel is testified to before all the world for a testimony. According to this the day of the Lord must no longer tarry.

You know, my beloved fellow members, how it is fitting to live godly and Christianly. Look out, watch and pray, that your wisdom might not bring you under judgment. Persevere in prayer, that you might stand worthily before the Son of Man. Be mindful of your predecessor, Jesus Christ, and follow after Him in faith and obedience, love and longsuffering. Forget what is carnal, that you might truly be named Christians and children of the most high God; persevere in the discipline of your heavenly Father, and turn not aside, neither to the left, nor to the right, that you might enter in through the gate, and that it might not be needful for you to follow an alien path, which the sinners, sorcerers, idolaters, and everyone who loves and does lies, must take. Be mindful of our meeting, and what was decided there, and continue in strict accordance therewith. And if something should have been forgotten, pray the Lord for understanding. Be generous toward all who have need among you, but especially for those who work among you with the Word and are hunted, and cannot eat their own bread in peace and quiet. Forget not the assembly, but apply yourselves to coming together constantly and that you may be united in prayer for all men and the breaking of bread, and this all the more fervently, as the day of the Lord draws nearer. In such meeting together you will make manifest the heart of the false brothers, and will be freed of them more rapidly.

Lastly, dear brothers and sisters, sanctify yourselves to Him who has sanctified you, and hear what Esdras says: "Await your Shepherd, for He will give you the rest of eternity, for He is near, who will come at the end of the world; be ready for the recompense of the kingdom! Leave the shadows of this world, rise up and stand and behold the number of the marked ones at the supper of the Lord, for those who have separated themselves from the shadow of the world, have received shining clothing from the Lord. O Zion, take again thy number and keep the reckoning of those who have fulfilled the Law of the Lord, for the number of the children whom thou hast desired is completed. On Mount Zion I saw a great host, whom no one can count, and they all praised God with song. In the midst of this host was a young man, taller in stature than all of them, who laid crowns on some of their heads, and was most majestic; I wondered and said to the angel, 'Lord, who are these?' He said: 'These are they who have taken off the mortal robe and drawn on the immortal, and have confessed the name of God. Now they are crowned and receive victory.' I said to the angel, 'Who is this young man who crowns them and gives the victory into their hands?' He said, 'This is the Son of God, whom they confessed in the world. Thus I praised those who stood bravely for the sake of the name of the Lord.'"[2]

Be warned, most beloved members of the body of Christ, of what I point to with such Scripture, and live accordingly, if I am sacrificed to the Lord; may my wife be commended to you as myself. May the peace of Jesus Christ, and the love of the heavenly Father and the grace of Their Spirit keep you flawless, without sin, and present you joyous and pure before the vision of Their holiness at the coming of our Lord Jesus Christ, that you might be found among the number of

---

2   Another reference to the apocryphal II Esdras.

the called ones at the supper of the one-essential true God and Savior Jesus Christ, to whom be eternally praise and honor and majesty. Amen.

Guard yourselves against false brothers for the Lord will perhaps call me, so now you have been warned. I wait upon my God. Pray without ceasing for all prisoners. May God be with you all, Amen.

In the tower at Binsdorf.

Brother Michael Sattler of Stauffen, together with my fellow prisoners in the Lord.

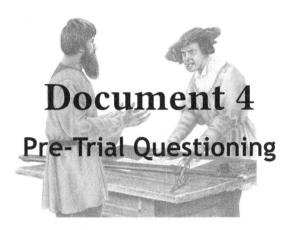

Document 4
Pre-Trial Questioning

This is the record of Sattler's pre-trial questioning. Many of the items appear again in the official charges. Translation from C. Arnold Snyder, "Rottenburg Revisited: New Evidence Concerning the Trial of Michael Sattler," *Mennonite Quarterly Review* 54(3) (July 1980):208-228, pp. 211-213. Note that the responses in this document are not necessarily Michael's own exact words, but were recorded by a scribe—probably one hostile to Michael and his beliefs.

$\mathcal{I}$tem, the replies of Michael Sattler from Staufen, a fugitive monk of the Domain of Hohenberg, given outside the trial procedure in reply to the articles of complaint legally brought against him by the officials of his Royal Highness of Bohemia and Hungary at Rottenburg of the above-mentioned Domain.

Item, regarding rebaptism and the baptism of young children; it is unnecessary and useless and merely a symbol; the reason is because Christ in the gospel said,[1] those who have faith should be baptized. Further, Peter in his first Canonical, the baptism is in you.

Item, regarding the sacrament of the altar, it is not the true body, blood and flesh of Jesus Christ, on the ground that Christ has ascended into heaven once, and sits at the right hand of his Father and will not return again to this world until the Last Judgment, as is stated in the [Apostle's] Creed; how then is one to eat Him? For this reason he holds that Christ is not in the bread.

Item, regarding the holy unction, he completely rejects it on the ground that oil is a creature of God; truly all of God's creatures are blessed and require no more blessing, and the popes and bishops should not bless such things further and thus hold their blessing to be better than God's blessing.

Item, regarding the Virgin Mary, the mother of God, and the beloved saints; it is true that Mary was a virgin and gave birth to Christ according to the flesh, but that the Virgin Mary together with the saints has to intercede for us is not true, for Mary is not yet ascended, just like others who have died, but rather she must await grace at the Last Judgment as surely as does any other person.

Item, those whom we call or name saints should not be named saints, but rather the blessed, for he is a saint who keeps God's commands here on earth and who, for God's sake, patiently suffers adversity, anxiety and tribulation.

Item, regarding the Turk, to whom he would rather belong than to the Christians, he would rather have the Turk than those who now call themselves Christians on the ground that the Christians of this time are now living in such a way

---

1   Snyder's translation of this paragraph was incomplete; the foregoing in this paragraph translated by John D. Roth from the German original in Lina Beger, "Wiedertäufer in der Herrschaft Hohenberg," *Forschungen zur Deutschen Geschichte*, 1882:444-447, p. 446.

that they should not be called Christians, and herewith the only Christians are he and his following.

Item, concerning the oath and obedience to our rulers, he answered yes, for one should be obedient to God and obedient to the authorities only in temporal things.

Item, that he left the monastery and forsook his habit and took a wife; answer: he had seen that the pope and bishops, monks and nuns were greedy, proud, envious, immoral and fornicators and full of evil; therefore he had not wished to be in the cloister any longer, and had married and hoped to be saved in this state.

Document 5

Charges Against Michael Sattler et al.

The official charges against Michael Sattler and his co-defendants. Translation from C. Arnold Snyder, "Rottenburg Revisited: New Evidence Concerning the Trial of Michael Sattler," *Mennonite Quarterly Review* 54(3) (July 1980):208-228, pp. 213-215.

Lord Mayor, by command of the noble Lord Joachim Count of Zollern, the Lord High Chamberlain and Captain of the Domain of Hohenberg, the officials of the aforesaid Domain of Hohenberg herewith appear before you and the Councillors and Syndics as advocates of the Roman Imperial Royal Highness of Hungary and Bohemia, Archduke of Austria, and Lord of this Domain of Hohenberg, etc., our most gracious and benevolent Lord and Royal Highness, in judicial contract, but excluding all legal contrivance, against Michael Sattler, of Staufen, Matthias Hiller, of St. Gall, Veit Feringer, Christoff Stainbrunner, Laurentz Schibel, Steffan Kreyssler, Martin Schopp, Matthias Geiger, Fritz Feringer, Ludwig Mollen and Jorg Koch as the men, and Margaretha, wife of Michael Sattler, of Staufen, Breida, Brendli's surviving widow, Frena, Conrad Scheupper's wife, Katharina, Martin Kreyssler's wife, Anna, Christoff Stainbrunner's wife, Salome, Lord Kessler's wife, Katherina, Ludwig Mollen's wife, Anna, Conrad Stotter's surviving daughter, Agnes Riemlin and Elisabeth, Martin Scheuppen's wife; and [we the officials] bring forward charges on the basis of the following considerations. Some time ago serious general admonitions and mandates were published by the highly esteemed Roman Emperor and Royal Highness in all of the Upper Austrian crown lands of their Imperial and Royal Highnesses. These same mandates were publicly read out in all places and towns of the Domain of Hohenberg before the entire community and posted on the town-halls and churches throughout the parishes so that the mandates could be read by all as needed. The advocates draw attention to these mandates and commands, as well as to all the regulations and statutes of the holy Christian Church[1] as held throughout all of Christendom. All this was included in the same mandates. Despite all this the afore-mentioned accused men and women have dared to establish a new sect and unchristian rite contrary to the holy Christian faith, contrary to all order and law of the holy Christian Church, by their own decision and against the published Imperial and Royal mandate and command. It is also contrary to their pledge and oath, by which some of them are sworn and obligated to his Royal Highness as their rightful, natural lord and sovereign. On the basis of their own unlawful initiative they have undertaken to destroy the holy Christian Church and to erect it [again] according to their unlawful, ungodly and unreasonable understanding. The ac-

---

1   The Roman Catholic Church.

cused have confessed their misdeeds under interrogation and torture. They did not disavow [their misdeeds] but intend to remain steadfast. [Their misdeeds] are as follows.

First, the above-mentioned persons have stated and confessed that in no wise do they hold or believe that the true body and blood of Christ, our Lord and Savior, is present in the holy sacrament of the altar, and also that man does not receive and eat the same corporeally.

Second, the afore-mentioned accused persons have created and celebrated a Lord's Supper, to the greater contempt of the holy sacrament of the altar. Particularly those from Rottenburg came together, put bread and wine in a bowl and ate the same in remembrance of Christ. They say, regard and believe absolutely nothing concerning the sacrament, as is noted in the first article.

Third, the accused persons have confessed that they despise and have absolutely no regard for the sacrament of baptism. Rather they indicate that such a baptism is nothing, that no one should be baptized unless he first has faith. They repudiate the baptism of infants which the holy Christian Church, following the declaration of the divine Scriptures, teaches, preaches and practices. Further they will in no wise agree and believe that baptism is a sacrament, but simply a sign. On this basis the afore-mentioned accused persons have dared to despise and disbelieve the baptism of children, and all have allowed themselves to be baptized again by an apostate priest, named Wilhelm Reublin, and by other persons who were in their society and brotherhood. They have accepted rebaptism against the order and laws of the holy Christian Church and have thus, as indicated above, despised the baptism of children. In particular Veit Feringer dared to multiply his disrespect for the magisterial authority by baptizing Hanns Lenndlin and Jacob Ziegler a second time, after Count Joachim von Zollern and the afore mentioned officials of the Domain of Hohenberg had arrested some of the accused persons for participation in these actions, in spite of all the warnings and commands of the government. In the same way Michael Sattler also dared to rebaptize several persons in the Zürich area and in other places.

Fourth, the accused persons have confessed that they neither believe nor accept anything concerning the sacrament of unction. They also despise the mother of God and all the saints.

Therefore the advocates proposed that you the Mayor and judges pronounce a judgment that is just, that the accused be sentenced to death according to Imperial Law, the law of the Holy Empire and as is just, having considered all exigencies.

Document 6
Two Kinds of Obedience

This is a Swiss Brethren tract of unknown authorship which has been attributed to Michael Sattler. It was bound with the Schleitheim Confession and other Sattler materials in some early Swiss Brethren tract/document collections. Translation from J. C. Wenger, translator & editor, "Two Kinds of Obedience: An Anabaptist Tract on Christian Freedom," *Mennonite Quarterly Review* 21(1) (January 1947):18-22, pp. 20-22; used by permission.

Obedience is of two kinds, servile[1] and filial[2]. The filial has its source in the love of the Father, even though no other reward should follow, yea even if the Father should wish to damn His child; the servile has its source in a love of reward or of oneself. The filial ever does as much as possible, apart from any command; the servile does as little as possible, yea nothing

---

1   Servant- or slave-like.—*AVS.*
2   Family- or son-like.—*AVS.*

except by command. The filial is never able to do enough for Him; but he who renders servile obedience thinks he is constantly doing too much for Him. The filial rejoices in the chastisement of the Father although he may not have transgressed in anything; the servile wishes to be without chastisement although he may do nothing right. The filial has its treasure and righteousness in the Father whom it obeys only to manifest His righteousness; the servile person's treasure and piety are the works which he does in order to be pious. The filial remains in the house and inherits all the Father has; the servile wishes to reject this and receive his lawful reward. The servile looks to the external and to the prescribed command of his Lord; the filial is concerned about the inner witness and the Spirit. The servile is imperfect and therefore his Lord finds no pleasure in him; the filial strives for and attains perfection, and for that reason the Father cannot reject him.

The filial is not contrary to the servile, as it might appear, but is better and higher. And therefore let him who is servile seek for the better, the filial; he dare not be servile at all.

The servile is Moses and produces Pharisees and scribes; the filial is Christ and makes children of God. The servile is either occupied with the ceremonies which Moses commanded or with those which people themselves have invented; the filial is active in the love of God and one's neighbor; yet he also submits himself to the ceremonies for the sake of the servants that he may instruct them in that which is better and lead them to sonship. The servile produces selfwilled and vindictive people; the filial creates peaceable and mild-natured persons; the servile is severe and gladly arrives quickly at the end of the work; the filial is light and directs its gaze to that which endures. The servile is malevolent and wishes no one well but himself; the filial would gladly have all men to be as himself. The servile is the Old Covenant, and had the promise of temporal happiness; the filial is the

New Covenant, and has the promise of eternal happiness, namely, the Creator Himself. The servile is a beginning and preparation for happiness; the filial is the end and completion itself. The servile endured for a time; the filial will last forever. The servile was a figure and shadow; the filial is the body and truth.

The servile was established to reveal and increase sin; the filial follows to do away with and extirpate the revealed and increased sin.

For if a man wish to escape from sin he must first hate it, and if he would hate it he must first know it, and if he would know it there must be something to stir up and make known his hidden sin. Now it is Law or Scripture which does this: for as much as the Law demands, that much more the man turns from God to that which he has done, justifies himself therein, by his accomplishments, clings thereto as to his treasure and the greater such love becomes the more and the greater will grow his hatred for God and for his neighbor. For the more and the closer a man clings to the creature the farther he is from God. The more he desires the creature the less he will have of the Creator. Moreover the law gives occasion to people to depart farther from God, not because of itself (for it is good) but because of the sin which is in man. This is also the reason why Paul says that the law was given that it might increase sin, that sin might thereby become known. Yea, the law is the strength of sin and therefore it is just like the servile obedience, that is, obedience to law, which leads people into the most intense hatred of God and of one's neighbor. Therefore filial obedience is a certain way through which man escapes from such hatred and receives the love of God and of one's neighbor. Therefore as one administers death, the other administers life. The one is the Old Testament; the other, the New.

According to the Old Testament only he who murdered was guilty of judgment; but in the New, he also who is angry with his brother. The Old gave permission for a man to separate from his wife for every reason; but not at all in the New, except for adultery. The Old permitted swearing if one swore truly, but the New will know of no swearing. The Old has its stipulated punishment, but the New does not resist the evil.

The Old permitted hatred for the enemy; the New loves him who hates, blesses him who curses, prays for those who wish one evil; gives alms in this manner that the left hand does not know what the right has done; says his prayer secretly without evident and excessive babbling of mouth; judges and condemns no one; takes the mote out of the eye of one's brother after having first cast the beam out of one's own eye; fasts without any outward pomp and show; is like a light which is set on a candlestick and lightens everyone in the house; is like a city built on a hill, being everywhere visible; is like good salt that does not become tasteless, being pleasing not to man but to God alone; is like a good eye which illuminates the whole body; takes no anxious thought about clothing or food, but performs his daily and upright tasks; does not cast pearls before swine nor that which is holy before dogs; seeks, asks and knocks; finding, receiving and having the door opened for him; enters through the narrow way and the small gate; guards himself from the Pharisees and scribes as from false prophets; is a good tree and brings forth good fruit; does the will of his Father, hearing what he should do, and then doing it.

[The church of true believers] is built upon Christ the chief cornerstone; stands against all the gates of hell, that is, against the wrathful judgment of the Pharisees, of the mighty ones of earth, and of the scribes; is a house and temple of God, against which no wind and no water may do anything, standing secure, so that everything else which withstands the teaching which proceeds from it, denying its truth, may itself finally give evidence that it is a dwelling of God—although it is now maligned by the Pharisees and scribes as a habitation of the devil: yea, finally they shall hear, Behold, the tabernacle of God is with men, and He will dwell with them, and they shall be His people, and God Himself shall be with them, and be their God, etc. But of the house of the Pharisees and scribes, it shall be said, Babylon the great is fallen, is fallen, and is become the habitation of devils, and the hold of every foul spirit, and a cage of every unclean and hateful bird, etc. But to God (through whom everything which boasts that is not, may be manifested that it is) be all honor, praise and glory through His beloved Son, our Lord and Brother Jesus Christ, Amen.

Document 7

On the Satisfaction of Christ

This early Swiss Brethren tract is of unknown authorship, although it has been attributed to Michael Sattler.
It was bound with early printings of the Schleitheim
Confession and other Sattler materials. This tract is well
worth reading and understanding, even though it may
take some effort to follow the argument at times. John
C. Wenger, "Concerning the Satisfaction of Christ: An
Anabaptist Tract on True Christianity," *Mennonite Quarterly Review* 20(4) (October 1946):243-254, pp. 247-254.

Paul says to the Romans in the third chapter, [that][1] they are all together sinners and
come short of the glory which God should
have from them, [yet] apart from merit [they] shall be justified by His grace through the redemption which Christ
accomplished, Whom God hath set forth as a mercy seat

---

1   Material enclosed in brackets was supplied by the translator to
clarify the original. Parentheses are original.—*Trans.*

through faith in His blood, by which He sets forth the righteousness which avails before God, in that He forgives the sins which took place formerly under the divine patience, which He manifested, etc. He says; From which also ye are in Christ Jesus, who of God is made unto us wisdom, righteousness and sanctification and redemption. John the Baptist says, [in] John 1, Behold, That is the Lamb of God who takes upon Himself the sin of the world. John says [in] I John 2, And He is the reconciliation for our sins. Peter says [in] I Peter 2, Who offered Himself [for] our sin on the tree, that we might be without sin. As the prophet also speaks, [in] Isaiah 53, We are made well through His stripes. Isaiah 9, A child is born to us, to us a child is given, etc.

Such statements, I say, and others like them, the scribes[2] interpret as if a person could be saved through Christ whether he do the works of faith or not. If such were the case, why then should Paul say [in] Romans 2 that God will render to everyone according to his works, namely eternal life to those who strive after glory, praise and immortality with perseverance in good works, but to those who are quarrelsome and are not obedient to the truth, but are obedient to the evil, there will come disfavor and wrath, tribulation and anxiety, [namely] upon all the souls of men who do evil. He says, [in] Romans 2, Not those who hear the Law are righteous, but those who do the Law. Paul says in Romans 3, He does not make void the law through faith; [rather] he establishes it. In Romans 8 he says, There is therefore now no condemnation to those who are in Christ Jesus, who walk not after the flesh but after the Spirit. For what the Law could not do, in that it was weak through the flesh, that God did and sent His Son in the form of sinful flesh and through sin

---

2   *Schrifftgelerten*, "Scripture-scholars." A term used by several early Anabaptist authors for the Protestant reformers, indicating that the Reformers, while claiming great scholarship and Scriptural learning, did not embrace the most obvious teachings of Scripture and even used their learning to avoid obedience.—*AVS.*

condemned sin in the flesh, that the righteousness which the Law demands might be fulfilled in us who now walk not after the flesh but after the Spirit. If ye live after the flesh, ye shall die. Galatians 5 [states]: In Christ Jesus neither circumcision nor uncircumcision availeth [anything], but a faith which worketh by love. I Corinthians 13: If I had all faith so that I could remove mountains but have not love, I am nothing. Ephesians 5: For ye know that no whoremonger nor impure person nor covetous man, who is an idolater, hath any inheritance in the kingdom of Christ and of God. Let no man deceive you with vain words. Ephesians 6: For ye know that everyone will receive from the Lord that good which he hath done. II Corinthians 5: For we must all appear before the judgment seat of Christ that everyone may receive according to that which he hath done with his body, whether it be good or evil. Peter [says in] I Peter 1: And since ye call upon the Father, who without regarding the person, judgeth according to each man's work so pass the time of your pilgrimage with fear. II Peter 1: And therefore offer, with highest diligence, through your faith, virtue; through virtue, knowledge; through knowledge, moderation; through moderation, patience; through patience, godliness; through godliness, brotherly love; through brotherly love, common love. For if such [virtues] abound in you ye shall neither be lazy nor idle in the knowledge of our Lord Jesus Christ. But he who lacketh these things is blind and doth grope. John says [in] I John 1, If we should say that we have fellowship with Him and walk in darkness we would lie and do not the truth. I John 2: Hereby know we that we do know Him if we keep His commandment. He who saith he knoweth Him and keepeth not His commandment is a liar. He who saith he is in the light and hateth his brother is in darkness. I John 3: Children, let no one deceive you. He who doeth righteousness is righteous as He is righteous, but he who doeth sin is of the devil. He who is born of God sinneth no more for his seed remaineth in him and [he] is not able to sin for he is born of God. I will not mention what Christ says [in] Matthew 4: Improve yourselves for the kingdom of heaven is come near. [He] saith to Peter and to others: Follow me. Matthew 5: Let your light shine for men that they may see your good works and praise your Father [who is] in heaven. Ye ought not to think that I am come to do away with the Law and the Prophets. I did not come to do away with [them] but to fulfil. Matthew 7: Therefore he who heareth my discourse and doeth it, him will I compare with a prudent man who built his house upon a rock. And then a pelting rain fell and floods came and the winds blew and beat upon the house but yet it fell not for it was founded upon a rock. And he who heareth my word and doeth it not is like a foolish man who built his house upon the sand. Matthew 10: He who confesseth me before men, him will I confess before my Father in heaven. He who loveth father or mother more than me is not worthy of me, and he who loveth son or daughter more than me is not worthy of me. And [consider] what He says of the good seed which falls into the good earth, Matthew 16, Mark 8, Luke 9: If anyone wisheth to come after me, let him deny himself and take up his cross upon himself and follow me. For he who wisheth to preserve his life shall lose it, but he who loseth his life for my sake will find it. Matthew 16: For it shall come to pass that the Son of Man will come in the glory of His Father, with His angels and then will He requite each one according to his works. [In] Luke 10 Christ speaks to the scribe [that] he should love God with his whole heart and his neighbor as himself; thus would he live. Luke 13: Strive that ye may enter through the narrow door. Luke 14: If anyone come to me and hate not his father, mother, wife, children, brothers, sisters, and also his own life, he cannot be my disciple. And he who does not bear his cross and follow me cannot be my disciple. He who doth not renounce all that he hath cannot be my disciple. John 13: I have given you an example that ye should do as I have done to you. If ye know these things, blessed are ye if ye do them. A new commandment give I unto you that ye love one another as I have loved you. So shall all men know that ye are my disciples if ye have love among yourselves.

Further, as Christ therefore hath suffered for us (He did not have where he might lay His head, Matthew 8) [must] we never through faith in Him renounce [our] supposed possessions and our [own] selves, and suffer for His sake? Why then does He say [in] Matthew 19 to the young man who asked him how he might be saved, If thou desirest to be perfect, go, sell what thou hast and give to the poor, and thou shalt have treasure in heaven, and come, follow me? Why does He say, It is easier for a camel to go through the eye of a needle than for a rich man to enter into the kingdom of God? Yea, why does He say [in] Luke 5 to Peter and Andrew (as was said above), Follow me? [And] to Matthew, Follow Me? Did not Zacchaeus say [in] Luke 19, after he [came to] know the poor Jesus and had received Him, Behold, the half of my goods I give to the poor, and if I have defrauded anyone I will restore fourfold? It would then be the case that Christ had lied when He says [in] Matthew 6, We cannot serve God and mammon. And that which Luke writes [in] Acts 2 of the righteous Christian Church which was once at Jerusalem, would not be true, But those who believed were together and had all things common. Yea, the article of the Christian Faith which says, A communion of the saints, would also be untrue.[3] Why then does He say [in] Matthew 8, He who wisheth to come after me, let him deny himself, take his cross upon himself and follow me? [And,] He who wisheth to save his life shall lose it. Why does He say [in] Matthew 5, Blessed are they who are persecuted for righteousness' sake [And,] Blessed are ye when men revile you

---

3   A reference to the Apostle's Creed: "I believe in . . . the holy catholic church, the communion of saints . . ."—*AVS.*

and persecute you and say all manner of evil against you for my sake, if they lie therein. Matthew 10, John 15: The disciple is not above his master, nor the servant above his Lord. It is enough for the disciple that he be as his master, and the servant as his lord. John 16: They will put you under the ban. The time cometh that he who killeth you will think that he doeth God a service therein. Verily, verily, I say to you, Ye shall weep and lament, but the world shall rejoice. Does not Peter also say [in] I Peter 2, For hereunto were ye called: because Christ also suffered for us, and left us an example, that ye should follow His footsteps. Yea indeed, if Christ therefore did enough by his passion which He suffered at Jerusalem, and nothing was uncompleted of his suffering, why then does Paul say in Colossians 1, Now I rejoice in my suffering which I bear for you and fill up in my body that which is lacking in the afflictions of Christ? II Corinthians 1: But as we have tribulation or comfort it works out for your good. Ephesians 3: Therefore I, Paul, a prisoner of Jesus Christ for you Gentiles. Philippians 2: And if I be offered as an offering and service to God [for] your faith, I joy and rejoice with you all. In the same way, did not Christ chiefly establish the Lord's Supper for this reason, namely that they had to suffer as Christ their Head, and through death enter into glory, yea that their death should not be theirs but the Lord's and that they like their Head should arise [from the dead]? And what about the dear apostles and prophets, yea even Christ Himself, and likewise the dear friends of God who suffer much at this time and who have testified for so many years,—if the members of Christ must not suffer like their Head? Does Peter not say [in] I Peter 5, Humble yourselves under the mighty hand of God that He might exalt you at the right time? Cast upon Him all your care, for He careth for you. Be sober, watch ye, for your adversary, the slanderer, goeth about as a roaring lion, seeking whether he can devour someone, whom resist, fortified by faith, since ye know that through your brotherhood which is in the world the same suffering is accomplished.

And for this reason when Paul says [in] Romans 3 that those who are justified through Christ are justified without any merit or without the works of the Law he does not mean that a man can be saved without the works of faith [since Christ and the apostles demand such], but without those works which are done outside of faith and of the love of God,—such as circumcision and the like, which the Jews did that they might thereby be justified. Therefore whenever Paul and Christ apply the term justifying to works they do not mean that those works are of men; but [they are] of God and of Christ (through whose strength the man performs them). [Those justifying works] are not performed by the man as if he received something as his own, but [they are performed] because God wishes so to give the man such works that they are His works. And why is there a mercy seat with God except for His own through His will? Why should God make known His will, if He would not wish that a person do it? Yea, how could God be satisfied with anyone who neither wishes to hear the will of God concerning His mercy seat, or who having heard and knowing thereof wishes to hold it only with words? Will he not diminish his boast that the mercy seat exists for his sake? Yea, he gives his own word and says that he heard it from the mercy seat. Yea, he curses and persecutes everyone who refuses to believe him. Will such boasting not lead to his damnation? But if we would think like Paul [in] I Corinthians 1, where he calls Christ the righteousness and wisdom of the believers or Christians, does he mean the outward Christ without the inward, and not much more the inward with the outward [Christ]? Namely, since He is the Word of the Father He makes known to us the true obedience by which alone the Father is satisfied. He is the true Bread from heaven which comes down from above to feed the souls of men. He says, He who doth not renounce all that he possesseth cannot be His disciple. He says, He who wisheth to follow me, let him deny himself. No one cometh to the Father but by me. I am the door of the sheep-fold. I am the light of the world. I am the way, the truth, and the life. He testifies all this in deed. I will not mention that Paul at this place is not speaking of Pharisees or scribes (as if they were the righteousness of Christ), but of him and those like him who accept Him in truth and keep their standing as His [disciples] according to that which faith eliminates and [that which it] demands. But what have they to do with it who boast to me so proudly of Christ? They allege that Paul wrote of them when they are the chief persecutors of Christ and of Paul.

How does it concern me that the emperor claims so many kingdoms, since I am a poor beggar? But when John the Baptist says [in] John 1, Christ is the Lamb which taketh upon Himself the sin of the world, he wishes to be under-stood: insofar as the world surrenders to Him in faith. And therefore he says also [in] John 3, He who believeth in the Son hath everlasting life; he who doth not believe in the Son shall not see life. In the same way also when John says [in] I John 2, He is our reconciliation, he wishes to be understood: namely, of those who so recognize Him. For although He is truly a reconciliation for the whole world, that does no one any good except those who recognize and accept Him by faith. And those who [accept Him] keep the commandments of Christ. But he who does not [keep the commandments] and yet boasts of Christ as being his reconciliation is a liar, inasmuch as he has never known Christ,—as John testifies. And do we think, when Peter says in I Peter 2, Who offered Himself for our sins in His body on the tree that we might be without sin, [that] he meant that Christ so offered Himself for the sins of men that through Him they are pronounced free, whether or not they believe on Him, whether or not they turn from sin, whether or not they have a change of mind, as the works-saints[4] and scribes think? That is far [from the truth]! Why then would he say [in] I Peter 1, Whom having not seen ye love, in whom ye also believe although ye see Him not. And whereas ye call on the Father who, without regarding the person, judgeth according to every man's work, conduct your life in the time of your pilgrimage in fear. Blessed be God and the Father of our Lord Jesus Christ who according to His great mercy hath begotten us again to a living hope by the resurrection of Jesus Christ from the dead. Now those who are without faith, who have not ceased [from sin], those sinning even worse than before, yea [those with] just as slavish and ugly a disposition toward God and their neighbor as they had before,—how can such people appropriate the words of Peter for themselves, since Peter did not write to them but to Christians? In the same way one understands also the two statements of Isaiah, for in Isaiah 28 God said concerning Christ, Behold, I lay a chosen, costly cornerstone in Zion and he who believes therein shall not be put to shame. The ruling Lord however shall be your fear and your dread, and He shall be to you for sanctification, for a stone of stumbling, and a rock of offense, for the two houses of Israel, etc.

How then did Christ do enough for our sins? Answer: [He did enough,] not only for ours, but also for the sins of the whole world, insofar as they believe on Him and follow Him according to the demands of faith, as was said. Yea, He has done enough as the Head of his church; He does no less for His members day by day so that He [continues to] do enough for those who are His; just as He has done from the beginning [so will He continue to do] until His Return. And therefore just as one speaks of justification through Christ so must one also speak of faith, [namely] that repentance is not apart from works, yea not apart from love (which is an unction), for only such an anointed faith as one receives from

---

4   Roman Catholics.—*AVS.*

the resurrection from the dead is [at all a] Christian faith, and [it alone] is reckoned for righteousness, Romans 4. Again, one must not speak of works after the manner of the works-saints, [namely], works of the Law, but [one] must preach works of faith, that is a turning back from works, possessions, and yourself through faith in Christ the crucified—not as though a man could do this of himself but as he is able to do through the strength of faith, so that these ["works"] are not of man but of God, inasmuch as the will and the ability to turn back to God are not of man but the gift of God through Jesus Christ our Lord.

Truly happy then is the man who keeps on the middle path and does not yield to the work-saints (who promise salvation or the forgiveness of sins through works apart from faith—that is through the supposed possession of works—and thus veer to the left, preaching works; paying no attention to a constant faith and not wishing to see or hear of a faith which is sufficient unto salvation: all their works are like wild plums, that is, ceremonies devoid of faith) nor on the other hand to the scribes, who although they have kept clear of [building on] works yet veer to the right and under the name of gospel teach a faith without works, taking the poor and obedient Christ (who had not where to lay His head, Luke 9, and without either the murmuring complaints or the defense of men said, Luke 22, Nevertheless, Father, not my will but Thine be done) for their satisfaction but they do not wish to hear what he says [in] Luke 9, Come, follow me. Luke 14: He who doth not renounce all that he possesseth cannot be my disciple. Mark 8: He who wisheth to come after me, let him deny himself, take his cross upon himself, and follow me. Yea, the Father must also be a "fanatic,"[5] [to] them when He says, This is my beloved Son in whom I am

---

5   German *Schwärmer*—a derogatory name used for the Anabaptists. The author is pointing out that God the Father insisted on obedience to Christ, just as the Anabaptists did. If they were "fanatics" for so doing, He was too.—*AVS.*

well pleased, hear Him. They make of Christ, in His humanity, what the pope has made of the saints, namely a golden
calf like the Jews of old, that is, they confess Christ as David's Son and [yet] they deny Him, yea make Him a "fanatic" because God's Word and Son were sent into the world to
make known the obedience or righteousness of His Father
not only in words but also with "works," so that all who believe in Him might not perish in their death but be delivered
from death. All their preaching and fruit are like prickly this-
tles; they have much to say regarding faith, and [yet] know
neither what Christ nor faith are; they reject works without
faith in order that they may set up faith without works. They
wish to obey God only with the soul and not also with the
body, in order that they may escape persecution. They think
that faith is a false and empty delusion. For this reason they
are able to say that infants have faith although they give no
evidence of works of faith, even when they come to years.
It would then be the case that the work of faith and of the
Holy Spirit would be cursing, when they are scarcely able
to speak. And alas for the miserable blindness, although it is
not because they do not know better that they do not speak or
write all this but because they wish to provide for the belly
and preserve their honor.

And how well can one see here the beast that hath sev-
en heads and ten horns, which hath again recovered from
its deadly wound, inasmuch as the Romish school or *Curia*
from which the bread-god[6] and infant baptism come originally, are again defended as the truth by the scribes. I will
not mention many other things in which the scribes hypocrit-
ically imitate the papists and establish them as Christian. But
thus must the second beast with the two horns—that is, the
gang of the scribes—cause the earth and the people thereon
to worship again the first beast, again establishing the papal
oil-idol,—that is, popery,—casting down fire from heav-

---

6   A reference to the Catholic Eucharist.—*AVS*.

en, banishing and cursing everyone who does not cleave to them,—everything just as John had said beforehand. This is also just as he had seen in Revelation 17 where the ten horns on the beast would hate the whore and make her desolate and naked, devour her flesh and burn her with fire, seeing that God had put it in their hearts. The kingdom would be given to the beast until the Word of God should be fulfilled. Yea, those ten horns who like kings should receive the kingdom after the beast, would be of one mind, would give authority to the beast, would make war with the Lamb, and the Lamb would overcome them. This is how there should arise scholars [scribes] in the last days from all the higher schools [of learning], awakened through the Spirit; and the Romish church or congregation of works-saints, possessed of great zeal, would bring everything on itself and burn up what it had accumulated of money, silver and food, and damn them [the awakened scholars] as heretics. But soon thereafter they would fall back to the beast,—that is, the Romish school,— and defend it, and the kingdom of God which had previously come to them they would again cast away. Yea these [apostate reformers] would defend the beast and those who cleave [to the beast], against the Word of God, and fight vehemently with the Lamb. Nevertheless, the Lamb who is a Lord of lords and the King of all kings will conquer them, together with [assisted by] His believers and called ones. And would not this, together with the papists, be the abomination of desolation of which Daniel in the ninth chapter, Paul [in] Second Thessalonians 2, Peter [in] Second Peter 2, yea also Christ [in] Matthew 24, Mark 13, [and] Luke 17, clearly have spoken, [namely] where that one sits in the holy place, allows himself to be worshipped either for gospel or for Christianity, according to which the works-saints say, Lo, here is Christ! The scribes cry, Lo, here is Christ! Therefore, happy is he who departs from Babylon, that is, [who] neither believes the works-saints nor the scribes, [but] submits with fear to the discipline of Christ, because the heavenly voice, [in] Revelation 18, Isaiah 52, II Corinthians 6, cries out and says, Come out of her, my people, that ye be not partakers of her sins, that ye receive not of her plagues, for her sins have resounded unto heaven.

Document 8

Ausbund #7

This hymn is attributed to Michael Sattler in the *Ausbund*, the hymnal of the Swiss Brethren. However, it is possible that it was written by Michael Weiße, a Bohemian Brethren hymnwriter, some of whose other hymns are included in the *Ausbund*.[1] Two metered English versions are found in *Hymns of the Church* (Benchmark Press, 2011) #532 and #592.

𝔚hen Christ with His true teaching
    Had gathered a small group,
    He said that each with patience
Should daily bear the cross with Him.

---

1   Ohio Amish Library, *Songs of the Ausbund Volume 1*, 2010 edition, pp. 56-58. Used by permission.

And said, you, my beloved disciples,
You shall be wide awake at all times,
Also loving nothing more on earth
Than Me and to follow My teaching.

The world will persecute you
And inflict much scorn and insult,
Driving out and also freely saying
That Satan is in you.

Now when men slander and revile you,
Persecute and beat you for my sake,
Rejoice, for see, your reward
Is prepared for you in Heaven.

Behold me, I am the Son of God,
And have also at all times done good,
Although I am the very best,
Still they have killed Me at the last.

Because the world called Me an evil spirit
And evil deceiver of men,
Also contradicted My Truth,
It will not let you off easily.

However, do not fear such a man
Who can kill only the body:
But fear more the faithful God,
Who can condemn both [body and soul].

The same proves you as gold,
Yet is gracious to you as children.
As you further remain in My teaching,
I will never leave you.

For I am yours and you are Mine,
Therefore where I abide there you shall be,
And who vexes you touches my eye.
Woe unto him at that day.

Your misery, fear, alarm, distress, and torment
Will be great joy to you there,
And this disgrace be a praise and honor
Indeed before all the Heavenly host.

The apostles endured such
And also taught it to everyone,
Whoever wants to follow the Lord
Should expect this.

Oh Christ, help your people
Who follow You in all faithfulness,
That they through Your bitter death
Would be delivered from all affliction.

Praise be to you, God, in Your throne,
Moreover also Your beloved Son:
Also the Holy Spirit likewise,
Who yet draws many to His kingdom.

Bibliography

MQR = *Mennonite Quarterly Review*

The Chronicle of the Hutterian Brethren, Volume 1. 1987, Plough Publishing House.

The Defense Against the Process at Worms on the Rhine. 1557, translated by Henry Walter, 2017.

Beger, Lina. "Wiedertäufer in der Herrschaft Hohenberg." *Forschungen zur Deutschen Geschichte* 1882:444-447.

Bossert, Gustave Jr. "Michael Sattler's Trial and Martyrdom in 1527." *MQR* 25(3) (July 1951):201-218.

Calvin, John. *A Short Instruction for to arme all good Christian people agaynst the pestiferous errours of the common secte of the Anabaptists.* 1549, John Daye.

Cook, William R. *The Catholic Church: A History.* 2009, The Teaching Company.

Fast, Heinold. "Michael Sattler's baptism: some comments." *MQR* 60(3) (July 1986):364-373.

Friedmann, Robert. "The Schleitheim Confession (1527) and Other Doctrinal Writings of the Swiss Brethren in a Hitherto Unknown Edition." *MQR* 16(2) (April 1942):82-98.

Friesen, Abraham. *Reformers, Radicals, Revolutionaries.* 2012, Institute of Mennonite Studies.

Fry, Timothy, editor. *RB 1980: The Rule of St. Benedict.* 1982, Liturgical Press.

Gregory the Great. *Dialogues.* Book 2. Translation from http://www.tertullian.org/fathers/gregory_02_dialogues_book2.htm (Accessed June 13, 2017).

Gross, Leonard, editor. *Golden Apples in Silver Bowls.* 1999, Lancaster Mennonite Historical Society.

Harder, Leland, editor. *The Sources of Swiss Anabaptism.* 1985, Herald Press.

Horsch, John. *Mennonites in Europe.* 1950, Rod & Staff Publishers (reprint).

Jackson, Samuel Macauley, editor. *Selected Works of Huldreich Zwingli.* 1901, University of Pennsylvania.

Knowles, David. *Christian Monasticism.* 1969, World University Library.

Lavater, Hans Rudolf. "Calvin, Farel, and the Anabaptists: On the Origins of the *Brève Instruction* of 1544." *MQR* 88(3) (July 2014):323-364.

Martin, Dennis D. "Monks, mendicants and Anabaptists: Michael Sattler and the Benedictines reconsidered." *MQR* 60(2) (April 1986):139-164.

Martin, John D., compiler. *Hymns of the Church.* 2011, Benchmark Press.

Müsing, Hans-Werner. "The Anabaptist Movement in Strasbourg from Early 1526 to July 1527." *MQR* 51(2) (April 1977):91-126.

Ohio Amish Library. *Songs of the Ausbund Volume 1.* 2010.

Packull, Werner. *Mysticism and the Early South German-Austrian Anabaptist Movement 1525-1531.* 1977, Herald Press.

Packull, Werner. *Peter Riedemann: Shaper of the Hutterite Tradition.* 2007, Pandora Press.

Peters, Greg. *The Story of Monasticism.* 2015, Baker Academic.

Pipkin, H. Wayne, & John Howard Yoder, editors. *Balthasar Hubmaier: Theologian of Anabaptism.* 1989, Herald Press.

Scott, Tom, & Bob Scribner. *The German Peasants' War.* 1991, Humanity Books.

Snyder, C. Arnold. "Rottenburg Revisited: New Evidence Concerning the Trial of Michael Sattler." *MQR* 54(3) (July 1980):208-228.

Snyder, C. Arnold. "Revolution and the Swiss Brethren: The Case of Michael Sattler." *Church History* (September 1981):276-287.

Snyder, C. Arnold. *The Life and Thought of Michael Sattler.* 1984, Herald Press.

Snyder, C. Arnold. "Michael Sattler, Benedictine: Dennis Martin's objections reconsidered." *MQR* 61(3) (July 1987):262-279.

Snyder, C. Arnold. "Michael Sattler's baptism: some comments in reply to Heinold Fast." *MQR* 62(4) (October 1988):496-506.

Snyder, C. Arnold, editor. *Sources of South German/Austrian Anabaptism.* 2001, Pandora Press.

Snyder, C. Arnold. "The Birth and Evolution of Swiss Anabaptism, 1520-1530." *MQR* 80(4) (October 2006):501-645.

Snyder, C. Arnold. "In Search of the Swiss Brethren." *MQR* 90(4) (October 2016):421-515.

Snyder, C. Arnold, editor. *Later Writings of the Swiss Anabaptists 1529-1592.* 2017, Pandora Press.

Stayer, James M. *Anabaptists and the Sword.* 1972, Coronado Press.

Stayer, James M. *The German Peasants' War and Anabaptist Community of Goods.* 1991, McGill-Queen's University Press.

Swan, Laura. *The Wisdom of the Beguines.* 2014, BlueBridge.

van Braght, Thieleman J. *Martyrs Mirror.* 1938, Herald Press.

Whatley, E. Gordon, Anne B. Thompson, & Robert K. Upchurch, editors. *Saints' Lives in Middle English Collections.* 2005, Medieval Institute Publications.

Wenger, John C. "The Schleitheim Confession of Faith." *MQR* 19(4) (October 1945):243-253.

Wenger, John C., "Concerning the Satisfaction of Christ: An Anabaptist Tract on True Christianity." *MQR* 20(4) (October 1946):243-254.

Wenger, John C., translator and editor, "Two Kinds of Obedience: An Anabaptist Tract on Christian Freedom." *MQR* 21(1) (January 1947):18-22.

Yoder, John Howard, translator and editor. *The Legacy of Michael Sattler*. 1973, Herald Press.

Additional sources for sidebars:

"Ferdinand I." https://www.britannica.com/biography/Ferdinand-I-Holy-Roman-emperor (Accessed August 22, 2018).

Bowler, Gerry. *Christmas in the Crosshairs*. 2017, Oxford University Press.

Crankshaw, Edward. *The Habsburgs: Portrait of a Dynasty*. 1971, Viking Press.

Graybill, Gregory B. *The Honeycomb Scroll*. 2015, Fortress Press.

Klaassen, Walter, and William Klassen. *Marpeck: A Life of Dissent and Conformity*. 2008, Herald Press.

Stravinskas, Peter M. J., editor. *Our Sunday Visitor's Catholic Encyclopedia*. 1991, Our Sunday Visitor Publishing Division.

Illustration credits

Title page—Michael Sattler's signature from his letter to Capito and Bucer. Basel University Library, KiAr Mscr 23a:Bl.2

p. 3—Anabaptism Begins. Art by Lisa Strubhar; © copyright 2016 Sermon on the Mount Publishing.

p. 18—Black Forest farmhouse. Public domain.

p. 19—Map showing location of the Black Forest. Public domain.

p. 20—Façade of St. Peter's church. Photograph by Andreas Praefcke (https://creativecommons.org/licenses/by/2.0/legalcode).

p. 24—Serf plowing. Public domain image from the 1400s.

p. 28—St. Peter's coat of arms. Public domain.

p. 29—St. Peter's monastery. Photograph by Taxiarchos228 (http://creativecommons.org/licenses/by/3.0/legalcode).

p. 32—Statue of a Beguine in Amsterdam. Photo by Dennis Jarvis (http://creativecommons.org/licenses/by-sa/2.0/legalcode).

p. 36—Täuferhöhle. Photograph by Doug Kaufman; used by permission.

p. 37—Weaver. Public domain by Jost Ammann.

pp. 46-47—Panoramic view of Strasbourg. Photograph by Didier B (http://creativecommons.org/licenses/by-sa/3.0/legalcode).

p. 48—Strasbourg cathedral. Photograph by Jonathan Martz (http://creativecommons.org/licenses/by-sa/3.0/legalcode).

p. 52—Michael Sattler's letter to Capito and Bucer. Basel University Library, KiAr Mscr 23a:Bl.2

p. 56—Title page of the Schleitheim Confession, printed mid-1500s. Copy at the Mennonite Historical Library, Goshen, Indiana. Photograph by Andrew V. Ste. Marie; © Sermon on the Mount Publishing.

p. 59—Inside the Täuferhöhle. Photograph by Doug Kaufman; used by permission.

p. 62—Schleitheim. Photograph by Wandervogel (https://creativecommons.org/licenses/by-sa/4.0/legalcode).

p. 66—Knight on horse. Public domain.

p. 70—Michael Sattler on trial. Art by Peter Balholm; © Sermon on the Mount Publishing.

p. 72—Horb am Neckar. Photograph by Felix König (http://creativecommons.org/licenses/by/3.0/legalcode).

p. 73—Ferdinand I. Public domain, by Jan Cornelisz Vermeyen.

p. 74—Rack. Photograph by David Bjorgen (http://creativecommons.org/licenses/by-sa/3.0/legalcode).

p. 82—Suleiman the Magnificent. Public domain.

p. 89—Sattler memorial stone. Photograph by Dean Taylor; used by permission.

p. 92—Anabaptist *Sammelband* at Mennonite Historical Library. Photograph by Andrew V. Ste. Marie; © Sermon on the Mount Publishing.

p. 97—Printing. Public domain.

p. 98—Ulrich Zwingli. Public domain.

p. 101—John Calvin. Illustration from I. Daniel Rupp, *History of All the Religious Denominations in the United States* (1849). Public domain.

p. 103—Santa Claus. By Thomas Nast, *Harper's Weekly*, January 3, 1863. Public domain.

Series

Also in the Cross Bearers Series:

March Forward with the Word: The Life of Conrad Grebel

by Andrew V. Ste. Marie
and Mike Atnip

Look for these future titles:

Jakob Ammann
David Zeisberger
and more!

Also by Andrew V. Ste. Marie
Walking in the Resurrection: The Schleitheim Confession in Light of the Scriptures

March Forward with the Word!: The Life of Conrad Grebel
(coauthored with Mike Atnip)

These titles are available from:

Sermon on the Mount Publishing
P.O. Box 246
Manchester, MI 48158
(734) 428-0488
the-witness@sbcglobal.net
www.kingdomreading.com

"For far too long Michael Sattler's contribution to the Anabaptist movement has been mostly the domain of scholars. With this book, Sattler's story becomes available to a popular audience. Michael Sattler may have single-handedly saved the Swiss Anabaptist movement from collapsing with his Schleitheim Confession, sometimes known as the 'Mennonite miracle.' Every Anabaptist should know and understand this story by adulthood. Each of us owes this former monk a sincere 'thank-you.'"

Chester Weaver
Teacher, Historical Researcher

"In this well written, scholarly yet highly readable, tome by Andrew V. Ste. Marie, the engaging story of Michael Sattler comes to life. It would be difficult to overemphasize Sattler's significance in creating, with others, the first Anabaptist confession of faith, the Schleitheim Confession of 1527—which, along with all other known Sattler texts, is also included. Sattler's Benedictine monastic background, often given short shrift in other published volumes, is strikingly fleshed out, adding real strength to this volume. A must-read for a new generation of Jesus-followers within the Anabaptist tradition!"

Leonard Gross
Executive Director emeritus, Historical Committee of the
Mennonite Church

"Written for a popular audience, this biography of Michael Sattler is solidly grounded in the sources. The biography is enriched by selections from Sattler's writings, giving the reader immediate access to his own voice. Its clarity of prose and passion communicates not only Sattler's life, but also the spiritual implications his story has for Christians today."

Edsel Burdge, Jr.
Research Associate, Young Center for Anabaptist
and Pietist Studies

Printed in Great Britain
by Amazon

73889039R00112